Managing Company

Providing a detailed break-down of the skills required to establish and grow a profitable production company, this book enables content creators and filmmakers to navigate the commercial video production world and the needs of its clients.

Drawing on professional experience in the industry as well as historical examples, author Tom Vaughan-Mountford illustrates the ways in which producers can avoid common pitfalls and better manage their business, projects, and clients. Making the corporate world accessible for filmmakers, this book covers all aspects of the video production process, equipping creatives with the tools – and the mindset – to offer their skills to paying clients in a reliable, repeatable, and above all profitable manner.

This book is ideal for filmmakers and content creators looking to establish a successful video production business, and features an online resource pack with example production paperwork including a call sheet, and example script re-write.

Tom Vaughan-Mountford has worked in the commercial video production and television advertising industry since the 1990s. He has worked in a variety of roles on several thousand productions, spanning a diverse spectrum of business sectors. Tom is currently the senior creative of a long-established video production company in the UK.

Managing a Video Production Company

Tom Vaughan-Mountford

Routledge
Taylor & Francis Group
LONDON AND NEW YORK

First published 2021
by Routledge
2 Park Square, Milton Park, Abingdon, Oxon OX14 4RN

and by Routledge
605 Third Avenue, New York, NY 10158

Routledge is an imprint of the Taylor & Francis Group, an informa business

British Library Cataloguing-in-Publication Data
A catalogue record for this book is available from the British Library

Library of Congress Cataloging-in-Publication Data
Names: Vaughan-Mountford, Tom, author.
Title: Managing a video production company /
Tom Vaughan-Mountford.
Description: Abingdon, Oxon; New York, NY: Routledge, 2021. |
Includes index.
Identifiers: LCCN 2021001935 (print) | LCCN 2021001936 (ebook) |
ISBN 9780367615512 (hardback) | ISBN 9780367615499 (paperback) |
ISBN 9781003105473 (ebook)
Subjects: LCSH: Video recordings—Production and direction—
Vocational guidance. | New business enterprises—
Management. | Business planning.
Classification: LCC PN1992.945 .V38 2021 (print) |
LCC PN1992.945 (ebook) | DDC 384.55/8—dc23
LC record available at https://lccn.loc.gov/2021001935
LC ebook record available at https://lccn.loc.gov/2021001936

ISBN: 978-0-367-61551-2 (hbk)
ISBN: 978-0-367-61549-9 (pbk)
ISBN: 978-1-003-10547-3 (ebk)

Typeset in Bembo
by codeMantra

Access the Support Material: www.routledge.com/9780367615499

Contents

About the author

Tom Vaughan-Mountford has worked at all levels of the commercial video and television advertising industry since the 1990s. Tom's career has encompassed client-facing pitches, scriptwriting, lighting, shooting, editing, audio production, motion graphics design, production logistics, production company marketing, and the management of production teams. The accumulated wisdom collected during two decades of working alongside many experienced professionals has formed the bedrock for this book.

Tom is credited for a variety of roles on several thousand productions across a diverse spectrum of business environments, from solo-enterprises to global businesses and government departments. He is currently a co-owner and senior creative at a long-established video production and television advertising company in the UK.

You can connect with Tom, and sign up to stay in the loop at *www.vaughanmountford.com*

Introduction

The commercial video production industry has undergone explosive growth during the past two decades. The traditional catchall "corporate video" is largely dead and buried. Today, the regular output of low-cost, fast-turnaround video—distributed via social media—is the norm. Video production for business purposes is no longer contained in its own unique silo. Video has been firmly established as a component of search marketing, social media strategy, PR, personal branding, and reputation management. Video is *the* go-to medium for businesses to convey any kind of commercial message.

The applications for video are so numerous that few producers setting up their own production shop can indulge in the luxury of producing only big-ticket "cinematic masterpieces," or work solely with a single variety of clients. Most small production shops seek to acquire a broad range of repeat clients. One-off commissions are just that, one-off. Being creatively superior to the rest is no longer enough to keep you ahead of the pack; the mere ability to produce attractive work is no longer the competitive advantage it once was.

The smart operators seek out clients with ongoing and regular production requirements. Consistently producing effective videos every day of the week requires solid business processes and a commercial mindset. You will need to be not only a talented filmmaker but also a shamelessly self-promoting entrepreneur. Video production is no longer a costly and infrequent investment. For many businesses, video is a daily consideration in their marketing and social media strategies. This need created a drip-feed of steady production work for those willing to invest the time and effort to forming long-term relationships with their clients.

On the flip side, the explosive growth of video has created a crushingly saturated market of youthful creatives brandishing cheap large-sensor cameras, and many will happily undercut anyone to get the gigs. Video production has become a hyper-competitive business filled with enthusiastic producers, often trading against loans or credit card debt while they produce work at cost or with minimal profit to build a showreel of work. During the past 12 months, six new production companies began trading in my city, an even split between solo operators and partnerships, and most of them under 25 years of age. If you have a mortgage or a family you are unfortunately stuck with a handful of fixed overheads, and these might be potential disadvantages you will need to factor into your business plan.

The role of the video producer has also transformed beyond recognition. It used to be the case that a producer's involvement ended with the delivery of an edited videotape and an invoice. Today, the remit of a producer is akin to that of a consultancy role. Producers are frequently called on to offer advice around online video marketing strategies, video search engine optimisation (SEO), streaming, YouTube advertising, Instagram Stories, Facebook ads, and analysis of the stats that stream back in when a video is being shared. During the past decade addressable advertising technology has reduced the entry-level budget for advertising on television, and a great many video producers have leapt on the opportunity to extend their offering into the creation of TV commercials.

So, while some producers *can* still indulge solely in the craft of filmmaking alone, most within the corporate sector need more strings to their bow, acting as a hybrid video producer, digital marketing expert, advertising agency, and a trusted confidante for their clients.

What motivated you to read this book?

I am guessing that your interest in producing videos goes beyond satisfying pangs of artistic indulgence. You might have already begun to develop your skills and have got some experience under your belt. You know that a commercially viable market for high-quality video production exists, and that—even in a saturated marketplace—you have something unique to offer. You have decided the time has come to get real and start approaching paying clients.

Despite your enterprising plans, you are primarily a creative first and an entrepreneur second. You might not have much experience with marketing, project management, client liaison, or bookkeeping for your production business. But you know darned-well that you must get good at these things pronto to stand out from the crowds of producers with "all the gear but no idea." A popular—almost romantic—image persists of the obsessive Hollywood filmmaker, agonising over every miniscule artistic detail. The reality is this: Top producers—whether they work in feature films or corporate video—strive to develop their skills across the board. They will not only know how to compose a great shot but also understand how the equipment they specify for a shoot will impact the profit margin of the production, and they will know how to build rewarding long-lasting relationships with their clients. The very best producers understand that—to capitalise on their creativity—they need to develop a rounded skillset that includes business management in addition to filmmaking skills.

If only you knew of someone with many years of experience in the video production business—someone to give you deep insight and coaching as you embark on your journey—well, hey, it's really great to meet you!

What you are going to learn

This book is *not* intended as a guide to teach an absolute beginner how to make videos, neither will it teach the specific craft skills of filmmaking. The best way to develop your creative abilities is to seek out work you admire and break it down. Figure out how it was done, and then have a go at replicating it yourself. That movie trailer you just watched, was there an overarching colour palette? What typefaces were used? Serif, sans-serif, bold, thin? What about the music, the sound effects? What was the duration of each of the shots, the pace of the editing? Learn this kind of stuff from the masters of the craft. Many DPs (Director of Photography), Colourists, and Lighting Technicians post behind-the-scenes Instagram videos of work in progress. Creative people love sharing their creative process. File your observations for the right moment to apply them to your own projects. I work with a DP who always brings a notebook to shoots. She is always poised to sketch the layout of a lighting setup and note the name of a lighting gel or a piece of grip equipment that has proved to be especially useful. Study, observe, record, and practice. Be a sponge for the technical processes behind creative works.

However, this book *will* teach you the fundamentals of managing a video production business. We will delve into administrative areas of the production process that I see—to my frustration—being overlooked or underappreciated. If there is an overarching lesson you take from this book it is this: When you broaden your business and production management skills with the same energy you invest in developing your creative abilities, your operational processes will become more refined, and the management of your projects far more professional. We are going to focus on the essential project management and business skills required to run a solid and successful commercial video production company.

Through the years I have witnessed many production companies and small creative agencies set up shop then go broke while still in their infancy. Often the quality of their work was impressive; but I suspect either their marketing strategy, accountancy skills, or client-liaison had left something to be desired—and, inevitably, the flow of clients and money had run dry. Put simply, a breathtaking showreel will not do much to impress business lenders; and no quantity of pretty industry awards in a trophy cabinet can rescue a tanking business from sloppy procedures or lack of financial controls.

I draw on knowledge gathered during my own career, complemented by the wisdom of many clients, colleagues, and freelance crew past and present. Currently, I am a co-owner and senior creative at a production company trading since 1983, a business with an archive of several thousand productions to its name.

The names and sensitive commercial details in illustrative anecdotes have been subject to adjustment; in fact, you will find a section of the book dedicated to the matter of client confidentiality. The anecdotes collected from various missteps—and their associated solutions—paired with the vast fount of knowledge gathered during almost four decades of production at my current business have never gone out of date. The valuable lessons are universal truths.

Today's youthful production teams often appear caught up in chasing the latest camera bodies, the most fashionable vintage lenses, and esoteric shooting accessories. Enjoying the newest tools of the trade—and figuring how to use them to maximum creative effect—is fun, but some of the basic "bread and butter" business skills acquired by producers through the decades seem to have been relegated in importance. Yet, it is your non-creative skills that will give corporate clients the most reassurance that you are going to act with professionalism.

So, let's get on with it!

1 Why are you doing this?

I reckon—gun to our head—many of us would admit we would truly love to be producing blockbuster movies, chart-topping music promos, star-studded television campaigns, or the next feverishly anticipated Netflix season, all with eye-watering budgets.

But think of the downside. We would have to give up quiet evenings at home to go quaff champagne with the stars at red carpet premieres and awards ceremonies. What an awful drudgery!

That said, the commercial video production sector continues its unstoppable growth and is no less of a career choice than Hollywood, or entertainment production anywhere else in the world. Filmmakers pursuing corporate clients must become comfortable with the commercial sensibilities required to walk the tightrope between pursuing their art and meeting the needs of their clients. Marilyn Heywood Paige is the Adjunct Professor of Marketing at the University of Denver, and Chief Marketing Officer of full-service agency *Paige Black*,

> Every creative person has to manage the friction between creativity and commerce. If you want to be free to make whatever art you want, get a day job, and create what you want on your own time. There are so many distribution channels now; you are no longer limited by being unable to get your creative work seen. The opportunity and possibilities are fantastic, unheard of 25 years ago. But, if you want to make money and have a career as an artist, you will have to compete against other artists—and there are thousands of videographers and filmmakers out there—you will have to bend your vision to the needs of the person paying you to make art. It isn't fair. I get it. Creativity should be unbridled, but when you want someone to pay for that art, their needs then become relevant. And there's the rub.

While writing this book I talked with founders of production companies around the globe. I wanted to gain a broader perspective on what makes today's commercial production business tick. Video is everywhere, and the quality spans the gamut from visually stunning and highly emotive, to painfully unwatchable. One thing *is* clear: Businesses have no qualms about allocating funds for video production. Video is the solution to a great many marketing and communications problems. Indeed, it is the medium that many consumers *expect* businesses to use. How much money those businesses might be willing to spend, and how much profit the producers of the videos will bank seems to lack any measurable benchmark; it is all open for discussion.

The video production sector is a highly competitive arena to play in because the barriers to entry have been all but removed. The upside of this is that there are countless directionless producers who have "all the gear and no idea," i.e. many of your "competitors" are not really playing in the space you intend to dominate. They might just be satisfying pangs of creativity while *playing* at business. Marilyn Heywood Paige points out,

> If you launch your own production company, you have to know more than just video production. You have to be able to sell and have a sales process. You have to be able to manage projects and people. There is a huge difference between running a company and being a creative.

So, if you are *serious* about *doing* business, you *will* be able to find a niche for yourself. Our business has a track-record of working for clients in retail, manufacturing, utilities, and healthcare; so, our team consists of as many planners and fixers as creatives. Our niche is the reassurance of rock-solid production logistics. To quote a regular client—speaking of another production company—"Sure, their work is very cool and a bit different, but we just couldn't trust them with jobs of the scale you work on." Perhaps your niche will be having a multilingual team, the qualifications to work in hazardous environments, or an understanding of a specialist industry that a competitor might not be able to get their head around. You should be capable of delivering great work for any client that comes through the door, but be able to excel in an area where few of your fellow producers will be able to follow.

The daily reality of running a production company is that nine out of ten potential jobs that come through the door will be relatively mundane, and many will be non-starters—never progressing beyond a speculative brief. I have worked on several high-budget videos featuring well-known celebrities, but those types of "prestige" projects form a very small fraction of the work that keeps the balance sheet healthy. It is good to aspire to create better work, and to chase more prestigious and wealthier clients. But temper this goal with some realism. Even when you become an established producer, most of your projects will not be destined for your showreel. Yet, those clients will want to feel they matter as much as those with larger budgets and loftier production concepts. Never give any client the impression that one of your other clients matters more.

Every glamorous project has been countered by dozens of productions about subjects such as sewage processing plants, biogas facilities, plastics extrusion lines, and beer-barrel washing systems. During the 1990s we worked with a paint roller manufacturer to film a guy in a lab coat rolling white emulsion onto a wall. Quite literally, watching paint dry!

On occasion you might find yourself working with clients whose line of work makes you feel uncomfortable. We have worked inside secure mental health institutions and operating theatres, and for several years we held a military arms manufacturer as a frequent client. Yes, even military hardware can benefit from a marketing video to demonstrate its "optimum kill probability."

The single point you should take away from this: There's rarely an ideal client in a creative sense. Yeah, you *should* pursue the dream clients that you'd love to produce work for; but never overlook the fact that—from a business perspective—an ideal client is nothing more than a reliable and genuine business entity that puts money in your bank account within your invoice terms, generates a profit for your business, and then comes back for more. Your dream client is almost certainly elusive and will have many other suitors in pursuit of them. Do not give up the dream; but remember that the strongest and most loyal clients are not necessarily the most exciting, or even the easiest to deal with. Many mundane and indecisive clients will readily pay for the exciting ways you can enhance their public image or the functioning of their business. Take pride in being the reliable expert who always does a great job for them, and keeps the needs of their business top priority, no matter what.

In summary

- Commercial videos are a means to an end. Meeting the objectives set by the project's brief is the service you will be providing for your client; the artistic process is intrinsically for your own enjoyment.
- Becoming an even better Producer, Cinematographer, or Editor might make you a more desirable freelancer for those *specific* skills. But, when you run a production company, clients will be commissioning on many other factors besides the quality of your work.
- Keep searching for the cool gigs (they are out there, trust me) but temper your search with realism. Accept that it will not be possible to love every project you work on. Be okay with that. Do a great job anyway.
- You will frequently have to work with clients whose line of business you do not find especially interesting. Find a way to become interested.
- On occasion you will find yourself producing work for clients whose objectives might be at odds with your personal beliefs. This is sometimes the nature of commercial video production.
- If a client settles invoices promptly and returns to work with you again, that makes them a *good* client, and you a *successful* business owner. It's that simple.
- If you ever cause a client to feel they are not your top priority, they will be entirely justified in walking away. Check your ego at the door.
- Find your niche; be it a sector where your skillset enables you to deliver truly outstanding work, or a variety of client you understand better than any other producer. This will be your area of competitive advantage.

2 Getting down to business

Structuring your business

At the outset I must make clear that I have always conducted business within the UK. If you are outside the UK, you should investigate the types of company formation options available to you. As with any business formalities, you should be clear on what the legal and financial ramifications are for you as an individual. However, there are three main ways to form a new business venture:

- **Freelance**. Sometimes referred to as being a *sole-trader* or *self-employed*. The "business" is simply the individual who is doing the work. If the individual ceases to do any work, the business essentially vanishes; the same is true if the freelancer takes a vacation. Crucially, the individual is responsible for any debts their business activities create. There can be many upfront outgoing expenses involved in the production of a video. If a client were to go bust without settling an invoice, any costs incurred by the project are going to come directly out of the freelancer's own pocket. For that reason alone, freelancing is best suited to specialisms where the individual is selling only their time and knowledge to fulfil a specific role on a production.
- **Partnership**. At its most simple, a business partnership is a legal agreement drawn up between two or more individuals doing work together (in the USA this is often named a General Partnership). The agreement will set out arrangements for how all partners in the business will work together—and how management responsibilities, ownership, the share of income and other assets will be divided between them. In the UK and USA each of the partners is still considered to be self-employed. Partnership law is complex and—in the USA especially—there are numerous variations of the partnership model. Few production companies are structured as partnerships.
- **Limited Company** (in the UK) or Limited Liability Company (LLC; in the USA). The formation of a business in this manner creates a "company" which is a legal entity in and of itself. This process is known as

"incorporation." Debts belong to the company, and the company's owners are shielded from liability for those debts. If a client were to leave an invoice unpaid, the company's bottom line would take a hit, but the founders would not be expected to reach into their own pockets to make up the loss. A Limited or LLC business can accumulate value (its assets, the money it has in the bank, and the goodwill of loyal clients), and it can be sold as a "going concern." When a Limited/LLC company employs payroll staff, the founders can sometimes take a vacation and the business will keep trading! But perhaps the coolest thing about incorporating a company is that you can give it a name, and no one else will be able to incorporate a business with that same name. Before deciding on a name for your company, you should check (if you're in the UK) on the Companies House website to make sure the name is available. Establishing a Limited company can elevate how clients perceive your business. Businesses that are seen to be properly structured can command sensible prices for their expertise. Countless business books can explain the legal requirements of running a Limited company, although they are not too arduous. In the UK, a Limited company may be liable for Corporation Tax and VAT (you can find a full guide to VAT here, https://www.gov.uk/vat-businesses), and your accountant will be able to advise you on the formalities. At the simplest level, a Limited company is a vehicle you can promote as a brand independent of yourself.

To work as a freelancer, you need do little more than to register as self-employed and take care of bookkeeping, personal tax, and (in the UK) National Insurance arrangements. Freelancing is a working arrangement that suits many video production professionals, though most freelancers tend to specialise in a single skill, offering their services as a Director, Cinematographer, Sound Recordist, etc. I shall assume you will—at first—be filling several roles: Offering yourself to clients as a total production service, and tackling everything from creative concepts, scripts, production logistics, filming, and post-production.

Some may disagree with me, but "freelance" can imply relationships that last only the duration of the project in hand. If you're going into business with someone else, subcontracting parts of the work to others, or even hiring your own team, you'll need to break up with the notion that you're simply a freelancer with a packed diary. When you work as a freelance hired hand you will only be building your own personal brand. To extend your reputation and ethos to others under your direction you will also need to be building the reputation of your business. It is a mindset change. In the enthusiasm of getting started many people get caught in the trap of brainstorming business names; buying domains; getting a logo designed; creating a website; setting up their Twitter, Instagram, Facebook, and all manner of other social media. Sure, these can all be valid tasks to act on when developing your business, but they do not in and of themselves *create* a business. We've all seen start-ups appear on our radar with a fancy website, an email blast to anyone who might listen, lots of activity on social media; yet we hear nothing on the grapevine about where this new business might be getting work from, or who their clients might be. Before long, the new kid on the block ceases to post updates, appearing to have gone out of business without even completing a single paying project. Getting caught up in tactics rather than executing on a strategy merely creates the public image of a business, with no real substance behind the façade.

As you're hoping to build a livelihood for yourself—and, perhaps others—by providing your expertise all the way from initial brief through to delivery of a final production, the nature of your role will need to be that of a business owner rather than a freelance creative. It is worth noting that larger clients—while they may bring in expert freelance consultants for certain projects—often prefer to award work to incorporated businesses (those with "Limited" at the end of their company name, or "LLC" in the USA) as this can give them greater legal recourse if anything were to go wrong. Publicly owned companies will sometimes stipulate a requirement for copies of suppliers' official reporting and ownership structure as a prerequisite for larger projects. Setting up as a bonafide registered company from the get-go lets you hit the ground running when you do eventually need to expand and bring other people into your business.

Employers' Liability Insurance

It is essential to have the correct types of insurance in place to protect yourself should an accident occur. Starting a new business is exciting. It is natural to concentrate on the fun stuff. But mistakes and disputes can strike even the most professional operators, even if they are not directly at fault. It is essential to have adequate insurance cover for the work that you are taking on. As an incorporated company it is a legal requirement to have Employers' Liability Insurance. This type of insurance will cover you against a vast spectrum of claims relating to accidents or illnesses affecting both your own employees and any freelancers you use. In the UK, this insurance is non-optional; you *must* have it in place to be able to operate as an employer. If you are forming a production company in the USA you should seek local advice as the regulations surrounding provision of insurance for your team vary greatly by state.

Public Liability Insurance

In the UK Public Liability Insurance is (surprisingly) not a legal requirement, but I consider it an absolute necessity. You will often be filming in a public place, or on your clients' premises. You might have an office that your clients can visit. Under all these circumstances there will be numerous opportunities to inadvertently damage something—or someone—no matter how careful you are. It is unlikely your clients will ask about your insurance policies, but when we have produced work for the public sector (or applied for tenders) our policy details *have* been requested. Local government departments often require a policy with cover of up to £5 million as a prerequisite for doing work for them. An annual public liability policy that would cover you for a mistake where you caused five-million quid of unimaginable carnage is relatively inexpensive. You can setup an annual policy online within minutes, so there are no excuses for not getting this cover in place. However, the requirement—and scope of cover—for liability insurance is not universal; you should check the corporate insurance requirements for your country to make sure your policy is appropriate.

Several years ago, we were called on to quickly film an interview with a politician. We arrived at the location, arranged the seating, and set up the lights. Midway through the interview one of the lamps began to smoulder (this was a time before cold-running LEDs were a thing) and within seconds flames began to lick out of it. We pulled the plug and made a dash for the door, lamp held at arm's-length, to get the mini fireball onto the street outside. Aside from leaving an unpleasant smell we managed to avoid causing any damage and went on to complete the shoot on schedule. No matter how professionally you conduct business it is always possible to become the victim of an unforeseeable incident.

Production Insurance

Regular office contents insurance can fall short of the needs of production companies. Policies can have many conditions and exclusions that producers can unknowingly fall foul of. Production Insurance is a more comprehensive policy that can often be bundled with the first two forms of business insurance when purchased from a specialist insurer. Production Insurance adds additional features specific to the needs of producers, such as:

Theft of equipment from an unattended vehicle: Many times there will be too much gear to carry in one trip from the car, and it takes only seconds for an opportunist thief to smash a window and snatch a case while you are setting up just a few feet away. Regular insurers may wriggle out of settling such a claim on a technicality, or the policy might only cover the value of relatively inexpensive items such as a laptop or luggage.

Professional indemnity: Indemnity cover can pay out in a scenario where you badly screwed up and a client needs to be compensated or has suffered a financial loss because of your actions.

Re-shoot costs: There are various scenarios where claiming the cost to re-shoot footage is the only option remaining. Let's say your camera gets stolen at the end of a shoot (no sweat, the camera was insured) but the memory cards with the day's footage were still inside (devastating—but also a reason why you should clone the data at the earliest opportunity!). Production Insurance would allow you to recoup the cost of the shoot—within the value the policy covers—and give you an opportunity to re-shoot the lost material.

Getting professional legal advice

A solicitor will have your back when you are confronted with a situation that needs to be resolved in black-and-white legal terms. In running your business there will frequently be times when professional legal advice needs to be sought. It is far easier to get access to advice quickly when you already have a good relationship with a solicitor who understands your line of work.

We required expert legal counsel when a track of music we had used on a production was later subject to a copyright dispute. We had legitimately licensed the track from a reputable production music library. Several months later a composer heard that same track in use on someone else's production and decided it bore a resemblance to their own work. The composer then put the wheels in motion to take legal action against the music library and, in-turn, everyone who had used the track. Our solicitor was able to step in and deal with the piles of legalese being sent to us and protect our interests. Eventually, the music library was able to prove there were no grounds for a claim of infringement and the composer backed down. Legal assistance like this does not necessarily come cheap, but it prevented a difficult situation from becoming far more costly.

Creating a functional workplace

The key word in the title is "functional." There can be a tendency in the creative industries to place workplace style ahead of workplace function.

Many years ago, clients were impressed by the clattering of videotape decks in complex edit suites. At one point we had a financial advisor who, after meetings with us, would sit at the back of one of our edit suites to watch us at work because he was so fascinated by the workings of racks full of whirring video equipment.

With video now being trafficked around as files, most small production facilities look little different to any other office. The novelty of visiting a production company seems to have worn off. This is especially true as the geographic distances between producers and their clients have become a less important criteria for doing business. For a while we had a client located in California—the other side of the Atlantic and several time zones away from us—and we would email and Skype our way through each project. From the client's perspective they would have been none the wiser if our headquarters had been a garden shed. They were happy with the results we gave them; our workplace was of no interest.

Create a smart and organised workplace that fuels your creativity—paint your office in wild neon colours if that's what gets you going in the mornings—just don't get carried away and blow your start-up budget on designer office furniture and Herman Miller chairs. Your workspace should add as little to your running costs as possible. Fancy office suites may be cool, but the lease on an office space in a desirable district can pile on the pressure to earn extra income just to cover greater outgoing costs.

Whereabouts will you locate your fledgling production business?

At the outset, your home is likely the best place to set up shop during the first few months. Working from home comes with a few caveats. Technology allows us to work from wherever we wish. Yet, from experience of working from home it can sometimes be a battle to maintain focus on the job at hand. This is especially true if family members find it difficult to understand that during working hours the home becomes your workplace. If you anticipate such pitfalls in running your business from home, there are cheaper alternatives to committing to leasing office space. If you are in an urban area you may be able to consider a desk in a shared "creative hub." Many cities have trendy districts where you will find coworking office spaces aimed squarely at creative workers who prefer a desk away from home.

Duke Studios is a coworking space in Leeds, UK. Fran Bundey, the Community Manager, explains,

> Duke Studios was born out of this very quandary, with the directors themselves graduating from creative degrees and not being able to find a place in which to work beyond their own home. We had artists' studios, corporate style offices, and boxed-off spaces but none of which were quite right or specifically appealed. So, the idea of Duke was born. Since we started in 2011, we have seen a huge number of other spaces open across the city and a huge shift in working patterns, wants and needs in the creative community as a whole.

But a coworking space is about far more than merely getting out of the house during the day. I asked Fran about the benefits of working alongside other creatives,

> At Duke, and a vast number of other coworking spaces, there is now a greater impetus on community and connections. A workspace provider's responsibilities stretch far higher than ensuring there is enough tea bags or toilet roll, it extends to fostering introductions, referrals, and collaborations between residents; from getting a quick snip of advice, to working directly on a major brief together. Encouraging collaboration is even built into the design of Duke Studios, with windows into studios and open doorways creating more opportunities for people to chat and work together. They have all been brought into this space on the same premise, as nice human beings who all work in the creative industries.

When I began my career, I had never heard of coworking spaces. Having recently visited several shared creative offices, I enjoyed the vibe. If I found myself in need of a place to get some work done in a distant city I'd prefer to do so in a more social setting; the feeling of "going to work" would get me in the right mindset to actually *do* some work. If I were starting over in business as a solo-enterprise hoping to grow, then sharing a space with other creative professionals would be a big draw for me.

> Duke was always designed to be an incubation space that small companies could grow-up and through with the support of the community around them. From coworking, up to permanent desks and studios. We have countless examples of individuals joining us as coworkers and graduating up as their company grows. It is something we actively encourage and support the best we can. Many of these stories are a result of contacts made and guidance and support from others in the space. It is the 'can do' attitude we aim to promote. In more brash tones of one of the directors, 'Fuck it, just do it!', which is arguably where we started.

The Flour Mill—a new collaborative creative workspace in Dundee, Scotland—agrees that a coworking environment fosters not only creativity, but also a growth mindset. Jerry Alexander of Liberty Space explains,

> We have had several members who have moved on to take private office space in other parts of the building. Some see coworking as a stepping-stone, and a way of keeping costs down whilst they work through a plan. They have always had the goal of getting their own space. Others gain confidence once they are in a coworking environment, lifting their aspirations to perhaps employing someone and taking on their own private space. Some simply want to work away from home in a creative and inspiring space, but don't want employees, just a great working environment.

The choice of whereabouts to situate yourself for optimum working is down to personal preference. Locating your business operation just footsteps from your bed is not going to be for everyone, even if it will result in the lowest possible overheads. As Fran at Duke Studios adds,

> The reasons our members so often give for joining us are for the company, community, conversation, a reason to get dressed, inspiration, someone else to make a cup of tea for, problem-solving, collaboration, or the need for a daily routine.

In summary

- Your production business can take several forms; however, the most common business structure is a Limited company (an LLC in the USA). An incorporated business carries with it more regulatory requirements, but if you are hoping to grow a financially independent business that can employ others, it's usually the right way to go.

- Your business will need Employers' Liability Insurance as a standard requirement, and Public Liability Insurance as a sensible addition. Check carefully for any other protection you might need in your country of operation.
- Regular office contents insurance can have conditions or exclusions that might make it inappropriate for the way you work. Specialist Production Insurance might be more suitable, and it can provide insurance against many more scenarios than regular policies.
- Develop a relationship with a solicitor familiar with creative businesses. There will come a time when you need legal advice, and it is good to know a professional who has got your back *before* you need to call on them.
- Your workplace should be functional, tidy, and make a good impression for visiting clients. The space should allow you to work comfortably and productively for long hours. But it should *never* add any more to your overheads than it absolutely needs to.

3 Working from anywhere

You might be surprised to find a chapter dedicated to remote working so near the beginning of a book about video production. Making videos is a very "hands-on" creative process. Imaginative creative work requires a bunch of people working together in the same physical location, be it at a client's office, a film studio, or chilling as a team on your office beanbags. Throughout my career I had become accustomed to doing business in just this way. Even on the occasions I would take a day out of the office to buckle down on a script or proposal, I would still return to the office the following day because... because... well, just *because*. A *real* business had to *be* somewhere; a gathering of people, a photocopier, and a heap of overpriced commercial-grade furniture, all located in a designated office space. In the previous chapter I outlined some of the options for *where* to locate your production company: A solo desk in your own home, desks in a coworking space, or even a leased commercial office.

Those were the most realistic options at the time of writing. That's just the way it was. Until it wasn't.

As this book was heading toward publication the world went on pause due to the COVID-19 pandemic. The filming of entertainment and movies went on hold around the globe, studios all but shut down entirely. Tens of thousands of production staff around the world were made redundant. As businesses shuttered their doors, they too put the production of advertising and marketing projects on hold. For many businesses, the commission of video content was—almost overnight—dropped to the bottom of the list of priorities.

As a busy production company, we were not immune to the pandemic's effects. Inevitably clients with upcoming shoots cancelled their plans, and projects we had pitched for were put on ice. Despite the crisis many of our clients speedily adapted and continued trading. So, we needed to find a way to continue delivering projects, even while our offices were off-limits. Like countless other businesses around the world, we had to embrace working as a remote team whether we wanted to or not. I was reticent to write with reference to COVID-19 as I did not want my research showing its age. However, the enforced abandonment of offices around the globe meant a lot of businesses—mine included—had to do the previously unthinkable and figure out a way to run their operations without a centralised headquarters. For some it was revelatory and became a natural evolution of their business; they never looked back.

I began reaching out to production companies around the world to ask whether a move to remote working had been a smooth transition for them. I also asked whether it might become a legitimate and accepted way to operate a video production business going forward. I received many largely optimistic responses. The positivity was not limited to responses from newly formed businesses. Established production companies also felt the traditional ideal of a fixed office space was diminishing in importance. Some even felt that locating a business in physical premises could be a burden and an unnecessary expense.

Muon Video create productions for growing companies in New York and Miami. Brett Cafferty is the Owner of Muon Video,

> I find the fixed-location ideal to be a topic of interest. I learned early on from someone much wiser that commercial space can be a hindrance more than anything else. The future is currently here. In the same way businesses learned from the 2008 crash that they could have a leaner staff taking on more responsibility, the 2020 COVID-19 crash will imbue businesses with a valuable lesson; that businesses can function with comparable efficiency, and save a lot of money, by working in a variable location setting. While it is atomizing, and lacking in in-person work culture, it is the way ahead. Workers, and communication, will become increasingly efficient with better tools.

One of the legacies of the pandemic will be the normalisation of running businesses remotely. Of course, many young businesses were already working with remote teams at the time the virus took hold. Phil Hampton founded Cartoon Media, an animation company, in 2012. Phil lives in the UK, but from the outset knew his business would be able to operate without the shackles of geographic restraints,

> We've never had a physical office since I started the company. I work with three freelance cartoonists for our Whiteboard Animation videos, all of whom work from home in their respective countries, America, and Hungary. One major benefit of working with freelance cartoonists is that I could attract higher-quality artistic talent than if I just limited my search locally. I also work with professional 2D animators and animation studios in various European countries.

I asked Phil whether Cartoon Media's clients take much interest in the location of his business, or indeed the lack of one, "Since 2012, I have met less than 10 of our clients, or potential clients, face to face. Hardly anyone asks whether we have an office or work virtually." Perhaps the proof of this statement is that when I contacted Phil to ask his thoughts on the potential for a rise in the popularity of remote working, I did not realise Cartoon Media was already operating as a remote team. Presumably, if I did not care enough to look for a postal address on Phil's website, other visitors might not look for location information either,

> No, they just see the quality work on our website and client testimonials and want something similar. Over half of our customers are based outside the UK, mainly in the US, so I hire freelance voice artists based around the world depending on customer requirements. I also work with a translation company and international voice artist agency if the customer requires non-English versions of their videos. We have virtual office addresses in the UK and US. We also have a virtual receptionist to take calls, and messages if I am unavailable. I pay for freephone numbers based in the UK and US which redirect to the virtual receptionist. Potential customers can fill out a contact form on our website if they'd prefer to send us a message rather than call.

I asked Phil how responsibilities are divided at the business, and whether anything would push them toward adopting a more traditional office-based model,

> I manage the projects, and write the scripts and storyboards for my regular animators, though I have access to freelance copywriters if necessary. I have tried hiring permanent staff in the past when we scaled, but it didn't work out. I found it difficult to manage multiple staff who all worked from home, but that may be more down to my corporate background, being more used to managing teams who share an office. If I scaled again and hired staff, I'd be more likely to rent office space. However, if I continued to work virtually, I'd make sure I hired a general manager, and used central project management software like Asana or Trello, plus virtual meeting software like Zoom, to make it easier to keep track of progress on projects.

Tracy Hagerman is Head of Production at June Day Productions in Johannesburg, South Africa,

> We are finding working remotely very easy. The wheels of our business are still managing to turn! I have been trying to get clients and crew to adopt a more remote way of working for years and, in fact, I had a regular client that I never met—even over video chat—for five years.

I asked Tracy whether the willingness of clients to forego meeting their production company in person might increase the likelihood of clients commissioning production companies at greater distance,

> I'm not sure about really global work at this stage. I am sure it happens but, with some of my clients, they still want to know that I am in the same city for context and basic cultural understanding. I work mainly with locally based corporate clients, so their training and corporate video needs are hyper-local in terms of culture and language.

While some corporate clients may still prefer to commission close to home, those sourcing creative solutions to their problems via the "Gig Economy" may be less concerned with the location of their chosen producer. Fatima Lagerås operates as a Creative Producer and Production Fixer at production services company Swixer, in Sweden.

> My clients are 99% international (non-Swedish) wanting help with their productions in Sweden. I have never been dependent on a physical workspace when producing or planning shoots. I am working remote all the time. I work with freelance-based teams a lot and typically I book them for shoots that are happening on location. So, to me, a physical workspace has never been crucial, and I love the fact that I'm able to produce no matter if I'm in Sweden or in Hawaii.

The most interesting of insights came from a production company with experience on both sides of the fence. Fat Free Media had operated within a traditional "bricks and mortar" corporate model, employing a large full-time team, before its Directors Neil and Kate Rostance made the bold decision to radically alter the structure of the business and close their city-centre premises. The pair now operate Fat Free Media, and manage their freelance team remotely, from their home studio in Nottingham, UK. Neil Rostance, Creative Director, explains,

> We decided to scale our business down earlier in the year. We completed the process a few days before lockdown started. Looking back, it was great timing! We had been running a larger production team, 16 at its peak, across video and animation. We had just finished our strongest year to date, yet we were fundamentally dissatisfied with leading a large production team, it caused a lot of stress. We realised that we just didn't enjoy leading a team. We decided to let our team go, and some of them have gone on to work with us on a freelance basis. We closed a posh office in the city and moved the business to a studio at the bottom of our garden. For a while we were genuinely worried that clients would think our 'big production company' was now weaker because we were working from a home office. Some of the bigger brands we work with are so used to lavish London offices, and their large advertising agency personas, even though it is largely just for show. We were really worried about not having that image anymore. Since COVID-19 hit though, I feel like it has given a whole new legitimacy and power to our new setup.

> The fact that we no longer have a big office to maintain is now a strength for two reasons. Firstly, we don't need to squeeze every bit of profit out of every job to pay for the big office. It used to be that we might want to spend a bit more time on a project to make it extra-special, but we were unable to because our margins were tighter. Now that we've got lower overheads, the flexibility to overspend on a project for the love of making great work becomes an option again. Secondly, we're not just 'coping' during COVID-19, we are fully functional. We have got all our assets, back-ups, network, automation, and hardware in one dedicated space. It's not a production company on the dining room table, we decided to make this our permanent space and it's genuinely given us a competitive edge. The larger 'production company' model is becoming less relevant as the years go on. It used to be that the guys with the big production companies with big rooms full of kit got the work, but now everyone has access to great kit, and everyone has access to the same software too. So, what is the point of a big office? What is the point of asking artists to come to work at the same place each day? Maybe it's about maintaining a consistent 'culture', but to me, I think the only reason physical offices exist in our industry is purely down to the speed of sharing digital assets. But, imagine if RED or Blackmagic announced a codec that made 6K footage the size of an MP3, we'd no longer need big server rooms and shared storage arrays, therefore we wouldn't need to be in the same space to access all our footage. Then what's the real reason we're all in the same building to do this work? A sense of company culture and morale is the only other thing I can think of that holds it back. However, the trade-off for a wonderful workplace culture are things like long commutes and stressful work life balance.

Neil also believes that potential clients' perception of what constitutes a "production company" in the traditional sense has been challenged by the pace of technological change,

> Some of the biggest content creators in the world operate from their houses. YouTube creators have shown that the classic 'production company' model isn't the only way to make magnificent work. The barrier to entry is not just lower, but completely fluid too. We are moving to a place where remote collaboration is not only more technically possible than ever before but is more accepted and championed by collaborators and clients. Working from home is no longer seen as the weaker counterpart to being in an office. I have thought a lot about the reasons why physical offices would still be needed and the biggest reason I keep coming back to is asset sharing. The pinch point for us, at present, is purely in asset distribution. Getting high-resolution video assets between artists and freelancers has been quite tricky. It has illuminated some of the luxuries of on-site media management. But this is only a small drawback compared

> to the benefits of working from home: improved mental health, lower stress, a better work-life balance.

Neil is positive that remote working can be a legitimate structure for someone launching a business from a clean slate, but adds some caveats,

> If graduates setting up shop can craft a workflow that thrives without the need for huge, cumbersome digital assets, then they will have truly achieved the freedom to work from anywhere. But with remote working, comes new levels of risk. Backup and data security become harder and harder to control when assets and projects are spread across different locations. I suspect there will be a rise in more entry-level DAM (Digital Asset Management) systems for creators over the next few years, along with products and apps that keep digital assets in the cloud with all the security and backup perks that come from having a physical office.

Tracy of June Day Productions agrees, and added,

> Yes, a new graduate could absolutely start a competitive video business remotely. This business does not require huge overheads when you can include hiring prices in your costing. Crews are booked and meet on location with their gear. My clients never come in for a viewing. Everything just lands in their mailboxes. My only challenge right now is getting location footage sent to me, we are still using couriers. I'm sure there is a better way, I just haven't made the change yet.

In summary

- Office space is costly and will add tremendously to your overheads. The marketing and advertising industries have a reputation for demanding fanciful "creative spaces" in which to work—it is legitimate to question whether you need to follow suit.
- If you can do most of your work on a computer, you are free to work pretty much anywhere you like. That said, temper your enthusiasm to become a roaming nomad—carrying a production company in your backpack—with a dose of realism. Working from anywhere could only ever be viable if your clients and the services you offer will allow for it.
- A decentralised business structure will require *everyone* to be kept in the loop and have easy access to *all* the information in the business. When the people working on your productions are not sharing the same office—or even the same time zone—they risk making assumptions about the direction of the project, or what is required of them.
- When coordinating projects with a remote team you will frequently be shunting multi-gigabyte folders via the cloud. Your broadband connection will be running full throttle. Internet Service Providers (ISPs)

heavily advertise their download speeds (and for domestic users wanting to stream 4K Netflix and run a 40GB update for Call of Duty, the download speed *is* the most important measure), but for commercial use, the upload speed is of equal importance. I would argue that connectivity should be one of the key considerations of where you and the members of your team should locate themselves during working hours. Working from the beach might appear to be living the dream; but as a deadline looms closer, no one needs the headache of frustratingly slow file transfers.

- Running a business with "no fixed abode" will require you to establish and maintain extremely rigid procedures for data management and backup. No matter where your team are located, all your production assets must be stored in a central location that is carefully administered. A production workflow that gets split across a handful of desktop computers, laptops, and mobile drives—whether they are a thousand miles apart, or just ten minutes away from one another—is a recipe for chaos. If a client were to urgently request a file that exists only on the local computer of someone who is sleeping on the other side of the world, you are going to run into problems. Your team can be decentralised, but your production assets must always be accessible to anyone at a moment's notice. I will delve deeper into media asset management in a later chapter.
- The newfound acceptance of remote working is more a method for collaborating with the best talent than an opportunity to travel. Sure, you *could* tour the globe while producing work for your clients, but it's more likely you might find yourself working in your local coffee shop while your motion graphics artist and colourist work on their respective parts of the project someplace else in the world.
- The mindset inherent to collaborating with a remote team can serve to broaden your approach to marketing your business. If many clients could not care less about your physical location, perhaps you should care less about theirs.

4 Assembling your team

Your production enterprise will likely begin its journey as a solo operation, or as a collaborative effort with a likeminded business partner. You might be able to spend the rest of your career as a do-it-all freelance filmmaker; deftly balancing writing, producing, directing, camera operating, sound recording, and post-production, without breaking a sweat—all the while *still* having time to find new clients. If so, which superhero are you? If you are consistently bringing in new work, you *will* eventually reach a point where you will need to decide how to adapt. There are three options:

1. Manage your workload by being more exclusive. Decline lower value projects or clients that do not interest you and focus on a manageable workflow in a tight niche.
2. Grow the business and continue to broaden your client roster. Focus your efforts on your core abilities and bring others to the table with complementary skills.
3. Give up the dream. Get a steady office job.

You will either take on additional in-house staff, contract freelancers for individual projects, or mould a flexible hybrid of in-house and freelance talent. Jordan Podos is the Principal of *See. Spot. Cut.* The New York company's website perfectly explains the "collective" working style that is growing in popularity,

> See. Spot. Cut. is a pack of media veterans who band together to unleash amazing work. Lead by Jordan Podos, the team is made up of dedicated creatives that jump at the chance to meet unique challenges and realise the potential of every project fed through the collective. We've abandoned traditional, one-size-fits-all pipelines that lead to formulaic results for an agile approach to team building that provides flexibility for clients. This gives us the freedom to nurture even the smallest project and ensure our client relationships are still spot on.

It was this description of the business model on the company's website that prompted me to get in touch with Jordan to find out how he formed a business with freelance talent,

> Nearly everyone is freelance. I, and one other Editor, are the only staff employees, with the 'first line of defence' being freelancers that we work with regularly and who always make themselves available. From the very beginning I surrounded myself with folks that I worked with in the past and trusted. You must be able to trust your freelancers to both be able to perform their tasks professional and in a timely manner, but also act professionally when in contact with clients.

I asked Jordan how new freelance talent joins his ranks,

> I only work with people who I know personally or have been recommend to me. Very often freelancers reach out, and I do have a conversation. I am polite but mostly but do not move beyond those initial conversations unless I am blown away by their body of work. [From there] The interview process is very simple. Typically, an in-person conversation and some light checking of references.

Although most freelancers maintain a conventional profile on LinkedIn, you can begin forming connections with freelance creatives on dedicated industry websites. The Dots *(the-dots.com)* is a networking site specifically tailored to the creative community, and it boasts more than half a million members around the world. In the UK, ProductionBase *(productionbase.co.uk)* is a long-established jobs board for freelance production teams.

Freelancers will come looking for you

Freelancers are continually on the search for new clients, and freelancers in the film and TV industries reign supreme in terms of the quantity of outreach they do to find new connections. When you establish a website for your production business, you will likely find the same. We typically get five to ten emails a week from freelance film crew, voice artists, motion graphics designers, and composers. Freelancers will often find you. Brett Cafferty, Owner at Muon Video LLC, is never short of enquiries; however, Brett looks for a specific pairing of traits in the freelancers he might want to work with,

> We organically attract freelancers through our SEO. Simply having a video company attracts freelancers; the pursuit is, of course, to find high-quality freelancers. The best advice to give to video companies is this: find talented yet agreeable people and pay them fairly. These individuals are far more valuable than you realize. You can always find

> talented people, and you can always find agreeable people. But rarely both traits are found in the same person. Compensate these individuals fairly, or they may walk.

Brett's advice chimes with something I was told years ago,

> Say you have a choice between two freelancers: a perfectionist who delivers sensational award-winning work but is a petulant diva who rubs everyone the wrong way. Or, someone who consistently delivers solid professional work, and is also affable and a pleasure to work alongside. Who would you rather work with?

You should also keep in mind that your clients will share the same mindset when hiring you to produce work for them. Marilyn Heywood Paige, CMO of Paige Black, regularly hires freelance creatives,

> The truth is, the person who can deliver what I ask for on time and who is easy to work with is the person I hire again and again. The person who has amazing creativity but cannot stay within the brief, deliver on time, or is too difficult to deal with I will never hire again. Even if their work is amazing. I simply can't. I answer to clients who keep the lights on. I have to deliver work that hits the mark on time and in budget, and I have to hire the person who will help me do that.

Assembling an in-house team

Conventional—outdated—advice for selecting and interviewing candidates often sits at odds with the nature of the creative industries. Most youthful start-ups (in *any* creative sector) need teams formed of original thinkers, and they rightly shun traditional recruitment guidance. Even when you are hiring for an administrative role you should be searching for someone with a creative nature that can complement your own (and that of your team). They should possess the artistic appreciation to understand what makes your business tick, and exactly *why* you are *so* darn great at what you do. Our team has been formed of people who pursued side-hustles in food blogging, fine art, DJing, screenwriting, and indie-filmmaking. Their creativity was not simply "switched on" for office hours only. Whether they were employed in a production role or not, their personal interests had a synergy with our line of work. We would share a *connection*; the relationship would just *feel* right. Trevor Rappleye is the CEO of production company CorporateFilming.net. Trevor says it is important to get to know the person behind the resume,

> When hiring other creatives, the worst thing you can do is hire them like any other admin worker. Creative people are hustlers, they don't want to

> be micromanaged; they just want to execute and make awesome videos. Chemistry is so important. My tip? Grab happy hour or have a virtual team happy hour to see how the chemistry is. When we hire, we look for two things: Are they happy, and are they passionate? If they have these two traits, everything else can be trained.

Of the few "bad" hires we have made in the past, the overriding reason the relationships did not last was because we hired for experience and qualifications above all else. All the successful applicants were well-suited "on paper" and hiring them felt the *logical* choice. In practice, the methodologies they had learned during their roles in other businesses did not transfer well to an environment filled with creatives. They possessed the *right* skills, but something on an almost unconscious level meant they were never entirely onboard with what we were all about. Requiring your candidates to share the exact same "passion" or "vision" you have for your business might be a somewhat unfair expectation, but ensuring they are on the same page—and that it isn't going to be *just another job* for them—is really important. Rob Level is the CEO of Smart Rapper, an online education platform for rappers and recording artists. The growing start-up attracts hundreds of applicants to every role, so Rob follows careful criteria to refine potential candidates,

> I show them the end goal from the jump. I am consistent from the day that I begin the interview process where I say, 'This is where we are heading guys. Don't attempt to work for me if you don't see this goal as well.' I feel as though I can teach anybody anything that I do—or have done—but I cannot teach attitude or afford to unteach bad habits.

The simple truth is, to hire exceptionally creative individuals, your recruitment process must appeal to their creative nature. To assemble a team that is on your wavelength, you need to write recruitment ads that would make even *you* tempted to apply for the position! Set the tone of the type of person you want to work with by carefully choosing the language you use. Regular job descriptions appeal to regular people. Your recruitment campaign should be vibrant, enthusiastic, and passionate. I was scolded by one HR professional for my writing style, being far too colloquial and casual to be taken seriously by potential applicants. There was a disconnect; they did not understand that I was writing to attract people who would be on the same wavelength as the team. A creative job description might attract fewer applicants than a generic one, but the candidates will likely be better suited to the role, and more aligned with the culture you are trying to build. If you are looking to attract candidates who are exceptionally video savvy, why not turn your call for applicants into a video and distribute it on social media? On the proviso that your recruitment process is entirely free from discrimination and open to applicants from all walks of life, the style and placement of your recruitment campaign can take any form you feel will resonate with the most suitable candidates.

Interviewing your candidates

Advertising a vacant position, wading through a tsunami of resumes, viewing hours of showreels, scheduling days of interviews, and then trying to evaluate the merits and drawbacks of a dozen equally likeable people are time-consuming and tiring. The candidates you bring to the interview stage should all possess the potential to *do* the job successfully. The interview is an opportunity to delve more deeply into the candidate's interests, their mindset, their character, and to further explore anything in their resume that piqued your interest. Meeting a candidate face to face enables you to get the measure of the unique—intangible—qualities that might demonstrate they are the right *person* for the role.

Open Google right now—I will wait—and search *great job interview questions.* I did just that, and it gave me 1,090,000,000 results. Any variation on the search returns hundreds of millions of results. The world would appear to be filled with gurus promising that *their* list of cryptic questions will get a candidate to divulge everything about themselves. Many of the questions in such lists make me cringe—they scream pop-psychology—or are worded in such a way that they would make a candidate feel awkward while they wonder what on earth the "correct" answer should be. Google themselves are infamous for posing extremely esoteric questions to evaluate the logic and methodology that candidates use. But you and I are *not* hiring for Google. Throwing a candidate off-balance by asking weird psychological brainteasers can be self-defeating. You will get answers, but they will not be of much use to you.

On the other hand, tired and formulaic questions such as "Tell me about a time you failed, and what you learned from it," or "What is your biggest weakness?" are so widely publicised on recruitment websites as to risk prompting rehearsed and unoriginal answers. Honestly—no one's biggest "weakness" is that they're a perfectionist who works too hard! Ask questions that are likely to provide genuine and intriguing answers that will be both *useful to you* and *relevant* to the operations of your business. If you would not be especially interested in hearing the candidate's answer to a question, it is probably too superficial.

You don't have to ask every candidate an identical checklist of queries (an interview should be an enjoyable conversation, *not* an interrogation) but there should be enough overlap across all the interviews to allow you to compare the candidates fairly. Here are some of the questions I have used that can elicit sincere and considered replies—

"What drove you to where you are today?"

This is a broader and more thought-provoking twist on the standard "Tell me a little about yourself." You read their résumé; you already know *what* they have done. You want to find out *why* they did those things.

"What really excites you? It can be anything, not just work"

If you ask about their hobbies, you will likely be given a list. You want to know what gets the candidate up in the morning, what really gets their adrenaline flowing. Do they light up with enthusiasm at the opportunity to tell you what really fuels them?

"Which project are you most proud of?"

Dig deep into *why* the candidate is so proud of the project. If they are simply pleased with the artistic merits of the result, that's fine. But it is especially positive if they mention how the project met the client's objectives, or if hurdles were overcome. If you are not interviewing for a production role, simply ask the candidate about their proudest achievement—either personal or professional. Finding out what a candidate is especially proud of can be a good indicator of what will motivate them in the future.

"What was the most awful, pain in the ass, project you ever worked on?"

This question can be the beginning of an interesting line of conversation. Note: Do not lead the question by asking how problems were resolved or what they learned from the experience, just let the story play out. Listen for the nuance in their recollection. Do they spend forever and a day bemoaning everything the client did to stall the project, or do they recount the steps that were taken to get things back on track?

"Which aspects of this role would you most enjoy?"

This question serves two purposes. First, it allows the candidate to indicate where they feel their strengths are. Second, it can give you heads-up on whether there is a disconnect between your description of the role and the candidate's understanding of what the role might entail. Maybe they are bubbling with enthusiasm about going on lots of shoots and meeting celebrities when this is simply not going to be the daily reality. Also, worth noting—*many* creative people apply for administrative roles in production companies to gain a "foot in the door" and later sidestep into a production role. If you suspect the candidate is, say, an aspiring Producer-Director, ask them if that is their end goal. This is an entirely legitimate career strategy on the understanding that the candidate is genuinely enthusiastic about learning other skills as they work toward their ideal role; but neither of you should be under any misapprehensions during the interview.

"Do you have an ability that you would love the opportunity to develop further?"

Asking a candidate about their perceived weaknesses supposedly provides an insight into their self-awareness. In my opinion, questions about weakness are flawed because positive responses can be so well rehearsed. Instead, ask about any untapped interests or latent abilities you might be able to help them develop. You can get a sense of their ambition and desire to broaden their abilities. This is especially important in a new business where you will initially need a team of flexible and multiskilled individuals ahead of recruiting dedicated specialists.

"What can you offer that someone else might not be able to?"

A strong candidate will be able to tell you exactly where two or more of their abilities or interests overlap to form a unique combination, and why that combination brings so much value to the table. The clincher that makes one candidate more appealing than another can often be a complementary skill, or personal interest, that adds value beyond the baseline skills needed in the role.

"What is your ideal working environment? How are you most productive?"

There is not a right or wrong answer. It is simply useful to know in advance how the candidate would deliver their best work, and how they might best integrate into your team. For instance, the candidate might say they are a focused introvert who prefers to work, unbroken, for hours with their headphones on. That is totally cool, but it likely means they would find it frustrating to sit with someone who likes to chat all day.

"Are you familiar with any other local production companies?"

Asking "What do you know about us?" as a rouse to see how well a candidate has prepared is something I thoroughly dislike. Their answer will usually—understandably—have some flaw or omission that will subconsciously bug you. I recall one candidate namedropping some of my past work, unknowingly mentioning (more than once) a production that I was far from proud of. Probing a candidate for their knowledge of your own business could result in an unintentional kick in your ego, at no fault of the candidate.

I find it far more interesting to explore what a candidate knows about the wider industry. It is certainly not a red flag if your candidate does not have an answer to this one (e.g. if they are changing industry, or have recently relocated) but being able to name a few competitors can indicate they have a degree of commercial awareness, or are tapped-in to the local marketplace.

"What is your must-see series on Netflix right now? – What's so good about it?"

Yup, this does *appear* to be superfluous small talk. However, you can gain an insight into the candidate's tastes, and the criteria they use to form an opinion on creative works. The question will also demonstrate whether they are able to connect on a social level. Are they able to hold an engaging conversation about something other than work? Can you imagine spending a two-hour journey to a client with this person?

If you've begun to get a good feeling from the candidate during the interview (i.e. they have made it onto the shortlist for the job) you should always introduce them to the rest of your team. Even just a couple of minutes of free-wheeling conversation with someone who was not present in the interview can be very revealing. Oftentimes, the candidate will be more at ease when the interview is behind them. Ideally, one of your team should also have been in the interview with you, to later offer their opinions of the candidate to compare with your own.

Attend graduate shows

University graduate shows can be a rich source of emerging creative talent. Many universities have film and animation courses, and graduates—while lacking corporate experience—will be overflowing with fresh ideas and enthusiasm. Follow the social feeds of nearby campuses to get a heads-up on the dates of graduate showcase days.

In summary

- When you gain a foothold and find yourself becoming overcommitted, you have three courses of action: (1) Carefully manage your workflow and become a specialist in your niche. (2) Broaden your client base and consider how to grow your team. (3) Give up and go do something easier. Only the first two options are recommended!
- For even the busiest production companies, there are peaks and troughs in the number of project commissions. Production teams must be lean and flexible. Most production companies employ just a core team to service their clients, while drawing on a roster of trusted freelance crew. Every position on your full-time team must be 100% justifiable.
- To attract creative candidates, you must create equally creative job descriptions that will appeal to their nature.
- A job interview is *not* an interrogation. An interview should be a friendly conversation where you aim to get the candidate to be as close to their genuine self as possible. You need to know whether you would enjoy working with them.
- Ask only questions that will get answers you are *interested* in hearing. Do not resort to pop-psychology or cryptic brainteasers. If you are unlikely to derive useful information from an answer, you are doing the candidate a disservice by not giving them the chance to demonstrate why they would be the right choice for the role.
- Chemistry is everything. Hiring someone with great skills whom you suspect might grate with yourself or your team is a recipe for the beginning of a problematic relationship.
- Go on the hunt for emerging talent at graduate showcase events.

5 The start-up shopping list

Do not be tempted to launch your new empire with a spending spree. Begin your business with the minimum viable investment required to be able to service your clients' needs. You should retain the start-up mindset throughout your career, and always be asking whether you really need to spend hard-earned money on a new asset or to make an addition to your ongoing overheads. You should always be striving to cut your outgoing costs, operating with as few expenses as you possibly can. Jason Cherubini is an accounting academic, and a cofounder of Dawn's Light Media,

> Many new business owners think they need certain things to be taken seriously, like a fancy office or an impressive website. These things can be nice to have, but they are far from necessary. By starting out operating at a lean level, and continuing to avoid 'comfort creep', your business can go from one profitable project to the next, without having to cover a large monthly burn. When our production business started, we were entirely project based, with no corporate level monthly overhead. We used our individual phones and laptops, with no company money covering those standard monthly business costs. As the business grew, we kept a similar mentality. At the corporate level, the only costs we incur are the few small legal, accounting, and overhead costs that are absolutely necessary to keep the business running. All other costs associated with the business are aligned with the projects that they are for. This way we do not have a large cash drain when we are between projects. This methodology helped us breeze through the shutdowns that were associated with the Coronavirus. While many businesses were in a situation that they were continuing to pay out business expenses without revenue coming in, our income statement was flat. There may have been no new revenue coming in, but there also were not any expenses that we were having to pay out. As businesses grow, this can get a little more difficult. The way we have dealt with that is we estimate our company overhead for the entire year, and we put that money aside out of our early projects. That way we know that our overhead is covered, and the business can then continue to operate on a project basis. Companies can operate on surprisingly little overhead if that is the way it is structured.

One of the largest upfront costs of launching a production business can be equipping yourself with the facilities necessary to create high-quality videos. Full disclosure, I *love* technology. Given the chance I would purchase every new gadget on the day of release. There are few things as uniquely enjoyable as cutting open the tape on a box, lifting out the polystyrene wedges, and inhaling the factory-fresh "new equipment smell." I get it, buying new gear is fun! But purchasing *anything* for your business must always be weighed against less exciting—but nonetheless essential—considerations. Buying stuff does not add any significant value to your business. Any accountant will tell you, the cost of all the equipment you buy will just sit on your business' balance sheet, where you will frequently be reminded just how rapidly it is depreciating in value.

Reality is that the latest and greatest kit soon becomes yesterday's technology, and not long after that it becomes entirely obsolete. The period between "this is cutting-edge" and "this is junk" will continue to shorten. Take it from someone who has been in the business a long while; most of the equipment I have purchased is not only obsolete and of zero cash value, but much of has been scrapped.

When I got into the business, technological progress was markedly slower. The industry was more standardised, and everyone bought much the same equipment. Broadcast-grade kit required serious capital investment, and we would keep purchases for a lot longer because they had to pay for themselves several times over. The gold-standard technology when I began my career was a videotape format named Digital Betacam. A couple of decades ago, a Digital Betacam camera had a price tag in the area of £25,000. What is it worth today? Nada. Nothing. It is junk. The hottest digital cinema camera on the market today with its gazillion pixel sensor and all manner of other cool new features will also be superseded and relegated to history. The lifespan of camera gear is especially short, and it simply might not be possible for some equipment to provide a return on investment unless it is paying for itself every day of the week. There is not such a thing as "investing" in equipment, because it will begin depreciating from the day it is purchased.

To buy, or not to buy?

Okay, so most production equipment costs a fortune and depreciates rapidly. However, there are undoubtedly a few filmmaking staples that you *can* justify purchasing outright; equipment that is so *inexpensive*—or will be needed so *frequently*—that it simply makes sense to have it in your possession. Your requirements will change as your projects become more complex; the more complicated the requirements, the more likely you will have to bring in gear you would not ever be able to justify purchasing.

Brett Cafferty, of New York's Muon Video, agrees with my "just the essentials" approach to purchasing,

> Regarding film equipment, I take a fiscally conservative approach. When you first start up, rent equipment for projects until you have an idea of

> who your typical customer is. After a few projects, you will learn what their needs are. When it comes to deciding on equipment, do not allocate too much money on cameras alone. Top of the line cameras are not a novelty anymore. The image quality gap between a $5,000 video camera and a $50,000 video camera diminishes every year. If you absolutely must own something, invest in lights, and audio equipment when starting out.

Marc de Vries, of the New York rental house Production Junction, also feels that a few items of basic lighting kit are useful to own,

> Bi-colour, or RGB, LED lights are a good option to buy for lighting. They can be cheap, battery-powered, easy to store and transport. So, by that rationale, you should rent HMIs and tungsten lights. These can be cumbersome and heavy, but a rental company might deliver directly to your set. Grip, in general, is better to rent [author's note: if it is heavy, made of metal, and is used to support or move something then it probably falls into the category of 'grip']. I would also recommend renting lenses, since there are so many options and they can be pricey. I don't think microphones get outdated as quickly as things in the camera department. If you are just doing smaller shoots, a shotgun mic is a good idea, and an on-camera monitor is also helpful.

Both Brett and Marc's advice tallies with my own. We keep just enough equipment in stock so that if a client were to ask us to shoot a simple presentation to camera at short notice all we would need to rent is an appropriate camera and lenses. We no longer have our own camera simply because our current clients have such a broad range of requirements. In the early days of your business, your needs will likely not be too demanding. You will be able to "travel light" and be inventive with what you've got. Get just enough equipment to meet the needs of most of your projects. Entry-level cameras with exceptionally high-quality sensors are frequently coming to market from manufacturers like Blackmagic, Canon, Panasonic, and Z-Cam; and inexpensive solid-state recorders such as the Atmos Ninja can extend their functionality still further.

Nic Weinfeld is the Founder and Executive Producer at Five to Sixty, a branded entertainment company with offices in New York, New Orleans, and Los Angeles;

> Starting out, it definitely helps to own some minimal gear, but don't blow your savings on it. You just want a simple setup that allows you to justify taking on smaller budget jobs and continue shooting [or] developing your portfolio without depending on new clients. As you level-up to bigger contracts, each job will require specialized gear, a specific camera, specific lenses and specific support. If you own gear, you may find most jobs demand gear outside what you own and thus you are just wasting a bunch of money and weighing down your overhead.

Mike Austin at LA Film Rentals (in Los Angeles) highlights that it is now commonplace to assemble the cameras and lens kits most suited to the project in hand,

> Every project is different and requires the DP's desired camera for the preferred look and feel of the project. Unless you are purchasing the proper camera for a need you have every day, renting is the more cost-effective way to go in the long term if you're handling multiple productions. Shooting photos? Canon or Sony. Shooting a music video or short film? Sony or the RED Epic Dragon, typically with EF lenses. Larger productions rent the Cooke lenses with one-tonne grip packages and supplemental lighting.

Mike at LA Film Rentals says making accurate cost estimates for productions can sometimes highlight where the purchase of equipment might be a cost-saving in the longer term, "Only purchase equipment that you will use every day. It's always best to budget out your production and see if it makes more sense to buy some [of the] equipment rather than renting for smaller items." For instance, we found ourselves renting lighting stands so frequently we purchased a couple of dozen of our own C-stands. The C-stand is a very heavy-duty lighting stand used around the globe; the design has never changed. C-stands are totally indestructible and relatively inexpensive. Ours have paid for themselves many times over. That said, we benefit from having somewhere secure to store our stuff; but if your production company is essentially yourself and your laptop, nomadically roaming wherever projects take you in the world, then it is perhaps not so practical to own any equipment. Mike at LA Film Rentals also points out a downside to owning any significant quantity of equipment,

> Another thing production crews are learning is when you buy a bunch of gear, you have to store and maintain everything. And if you don't get insurance on your own gear and something happens, you're out [the cost of] that gear.

I can personally endorse Mike's advice on that point; I lost a camera and a location audio mixer to an opportunistic thief. Even though the items were insured, the insurer refused to pay on a technicality, so in that instance—even with what appeared to be adequate precautions in place—owning our own equipment proved a costly liability.

So, when your own equipment cannot meet the requirements of a more complex production, how—and why—might you choose to rent it?

Equipment rental—all the latest toys, without the financial baggage

Relentless innovation in filmmaking equipment has brought so many options to market that many production companies rely on knowledgeable rental companies to assemble appropriate packages of equipment. If you are located anywhere near a metropolitan area, you will have a large selection of gear available on your doorstep. So, starting out your production company without a piece of filming kit to your name is entirely feasible (if not sensible).

Brad Wilson is the Vice President of Business Development at Keslow Camera, a large equipment rental company with bases across the USA, catering for the requirements of every tier of production including major feature films,

> Most production companies will be better off renting to begin with. You require less capital upfront, and you have less overhead and gear to maintain, etc. Not only that, but said gear you did end up purchasing could become obsolete sooner than you may realize, and you won't want to worry about the hassle of selling and purchasing new equipment to remain at the cutting-edge of technology, whereas a rental house would have those channels worked out.

Beyond the obvious benefit of letting someone else take the financial hit if the gear becomes obsolete, rental can also broaden your creative options. Prior to the ever-changing landscape of digital cinema gear, we owned a standard off-the-shelf broadcast camera, and we felt obligated to use it for every shoot. Looking back at our work from that time, it had an overarching similar "look" that was inherent to the camera model. Whereas, today, you can tailor your shooting package to achieve whatever style the project demands. Marc, at Production Junction, agrees

> Different productions will have different specs, and there isn't a one-size-fits-all camera out there. You can buy the greatest 4K camera and cinema lenses for your money today, but if next year everyone is looking for films to be shot in 6K, or a client wants a look your lenses don't do, you might wish you had waited, or had stuck to renting. Lighting could be the same; if a manufacturer puts out a light that lasts 4 hours on battery, has more output, a colour spectrum closer to an HMI, etc. I'm not saying no gear is worth buying, but these are some examples of the rental philosophy. Rental houses also offer accessories and more esoteric grip items that can make your shoots easier, and we also offer advice and technical support, should you need it.

If you do opt to purchase items of your own equipment, keep in mind they will likely only get used by yourself, and any staff you employ. If you bring in a freelance crew, it's likely they will prefer to either use their own equipment or will help you specify what rental kit they require for the project. Brad at Keslow Camera explains how this usually plays out,

> Producers for studios or running larger productions typically defer to their cinematographer on where they source their gear, and usually the

cinematographer will choose to use a rental house because of the myriad of options and depth that a rental house would offer in terms of camera and lens choices, as opposed to an otherwise small arsenal that an individual could typically purchase with their own money. Not only that, but a rental house will have backups upon backups of gear in case anything goes down during the shoot or is damaged during production. Lastly, but perhaps as importantly, traditional rental houses provide access to highly trained technicians on call 24/7 to ensure everything is running throughout the shoot, which I'm sure provides a nice stress relief for most.

Equipment rental—be a good client

We have found equipment rental houses are most amenable to cutting deals, arranging training, or swiftly arranging an eleventh-hour booking when they feel you are a loyal client. I cannot overstate the importance of being a good client to businesses and individuals to whom you subcontract aspects of your productions. When you find yourself in a tight spot, or need something at the last minute, you will want to be the person with a positive reputation that others will want to go the extra mile to help. Keslow's Brad points out that it pays dividends to build and maintain a close relationship with your rental shop,

> I would recommend reaching out to the rental house and setting up a meeting in person to begin a relationship with a certain individual there who will become your account manager. Quickly fill out their application forms and abide by their terms and conditions, get them a current certificate of insurance, and then start driving business to that rental house. The stronger the personal relationship you build, and the more business you bring to them, the more leverage you'll have in negotiating rental rates with them, which will in turn bring you maximum value.

Don't miss the opportunity to learn

Be sure to follow the social media and newsletters of your nearby rental shops. Many of them will run open-days and training sessions for recent additions to their equipment armoury. When a new piece of gear hits the market, your rental shop is often the first place where crews can get hands-on experience of using it. There will also be people on hand who have studied the new equipment in-depth; they will be familiar with its quirks, and tricks to get the best performance from the kit, working knowledge that is not in the instruction manuals! While all rental companies will deliver equipment to you, Marc at Production Junction recommends getting up to speed on unfamiliar equipment ahead of time,

> Plan for a check-out session. We allow our clients to come into our office early to test out gear and build rigs. This will let you root out any possible

> problems ahead of time, and it will also help you understand your options. We have taught clients how to use gimbals, EasyRigs, and Teradek systems right in the office.

Dave Bardsley of Media Dog—an equipment rental firm headquartered in Manchester, UK—also raised an observation that I hadn't yet considered; purchasing and relying solely on nothing more than your own small assembly of equipment could limit your creative options, and also cause you to miss the opportunity to learn from the experience of others,

> I've been doing this for over 14 years, and I have noticed a change in the quality of new crew. People used to work their way up the ladder, start as a runner, then move up to clapper loading etc. Now, you get people who have bought themselves a DSLR or a Blackmagic and they are now [calling themselves] a Director of Photography, going straight to the top without gaining any experience along the way. This will never be the correct way to do things. The art of film will be lost, there are many things you can and will learn from your peers. They have worked their way up and have learned how things used to be shot, and the techniques they used to create an effect without proper equipment. This is an invaluable process. People do not want to start at the bottom, some think its beneath them. They should relish in the challenge and gain their own skills along the way this would make them more rounded as a filmmaker.

How does rental work?

Imagine you own a Ferrari. Perhaps your production company became an overnight success (you're welcome!). Would you just hand over your keys to a stranger who tells you they are responsible, and promises to return it undamaged? Nope.

I will give you some perspective. Let us say your client wants to achieve a highly cinematic style for a video to market their brand on a global scale. Using your personal entry-level camera and small LED lights might not be able to deliver the results they want. This project is going to require a top-level camera, a set of primes, and a follow-focus rig. HMIs (metal-halide gas discharge lamps) might be required to achieve the lighting style the client wants. And, if you are not getting the rental firm to deliver the gear to your filming location, you might also need to hire a vehicle to move it all around. With a single commission you could leap from being responsible for £5,000 of your own equipment, to shouldering responsibility for £100,000 of someone else's.

Before you start having sleepless nights about the value of the gear required for your projects, fear not. Your rental house has the situation all worked out. They understand no two bookings are going to be the same, and the insurance criteria will vary greatly. Ask your account manager for their guidance.

Here are some of the most likely criteria any rental company will require you to meet:

> You will need to provide photographic ID. As I said, you would not lend your Ferrari to a total stranger. If you have not rented before, and are needing to take out a substantial amount of equipment, you might also be asked to provide a reference (another reason why it's worthwhile getting to know plenty of people in the business!) Mike at LA Film Rentals adds, "It's also smart to keep your social media and IMDB profile updated as we [also] use that for verification purposes."

The equipment will need to be covered by insurance throughout the rental period. Insurers specialising in film and television production insurance offer policies to cover equipment while it is in your possession. They can arrange short-term policies for the period of your production (even if that's just a few days) for the value of the equipment you are renting. If you regularly rent equipment, insurers can arrange annual policies to cover rented equipment up to a set value. Unsurprisingly, you will need to provide details of the policy you have in place to the rental shop.

Rental houses will require a credit card authorisation on any rental. They will often ask to hold an amount equivalent to the excess on the insurance policy you have put in place (the excess is any shortfall the policy won't pay for, in the USA this is known as the "deductible"). The hold on the credit card will enable the rental shop to cover their immediate expenses if any gear gets lost or damaged, or if you fail to settle their invoice. Important tip: If you want to continue using other people's expensive gear, NEVER do any of those things!

Marc de Vries at Production Junction, New York, adds,

> Renters can also opt to purchase a damage waiver, which is similar to short-term insurance policies in terms of price, but is really only beneficial for when the gear's total value is under $20,000. Should it not be possible to use insurance, and a damage waiver won't work for them, renters can just have us run a credit card hold for 80% of the total value of the equipment rented. Just be ready to fill out paperwork and provide us the info we crave! Insurance, payment info, references… the sooner those get taken care of, the sooner we can prepare the gear and get it over to you.

In summary

- Even the best equipment in the world is just inanimate "stuff." In and of itself, great equipment does not by default create a great business. Anyone with a credit card or a loan can buy superb equipment—but when no clients are giving them paying work, those folks will *still* be paying for their purchases!

- An entry-level camera and a few other staple items of production equipment can be sensible purchases on the proviso that they will be continually used, are relatively inexpensive, and are unlikely to be made obsolete in the longer-term (or are unlikely to *ever* go out of date).
- Consider what is an essential purchase, and what is not. Do your sums first to make sure the equipment will have paid its way long before it starts to become obsolete.
- If you do purchase any of your own equipment, make sure you have somewhere secure to store it. Make sure your kit is adequately insured, and check your policy carefully for any specific security requirements you should put in place.
- Clearly mark your equipment so it is *easily* identifiable as yours, otherwise it *will* eventually go missing in action when someone packs it with rental kit or puts it in someone else's car.
- Renting equipment is commonplace, especially for small production teams or anyone working from home or remotely. The same equipment used to shoot major feature films is also yours to use, and when you are not using it—it is not costing you anything.
- Become your rental provider's best client. Rental shops appreciate every shoot is going to be different, so there is scope for negotiation on price—*if* you are a loyal client.
- Experienced rental providers do not just ship boxes of equipment, they understand filmmaking and how to get the best results from the kit; listen to their wisdom!
- A good rental shop will always have your back and, if any fault arises, they will have a plan of action to keep your production on track.
- Research insurers that specialise in cover for production companies. It is very unlikely that personal or general business insurance policies are going to cover equipment under your temporary care.
- If an item of equipment is expensive, likely to be superseded, and you are using it infrequently—get to know a good rental house.

6 Promoting your business

Here it is. The chapter from hell. This has been the most daunting part of the book to write. How so? Well, proponents of every advertising medium will insist theirs is the most effective channel to raise a crowd of frenzied clients beating a path to your door. So, whatever type of advertising I endorse or critique, I am going to take some flak. They will all be wrong of course! You and I both know that video is the one and only undisputed medium to slay them all.

The difference between advertising and marketing

Before we embark, I shall clarify two important words that often get used interchangeably: Advertising and marketing.

Marketing is the process of gathering information on your intended consumer, then shaping your offering to perfectly meet their requirements. Marketing can include (but certainly isn't limited to) the name of your business, how you present yourself, the language you use in your emails, the design of your website, the type of images you post on your Instagram; and of course, the style of the work you produce, and what you're charging for it. Marketing is all the background work you do to shape the thoughts and feelings a potential client may form about you and your business. Your marketing activities should all be working together to align your production business with the needs of prospective clients. This is known as *brand positioning* (yeah, it sounds a bit pretentious, but every successful business does this—whether they use the term or not).

Advertising is a *part* of the marketing process. Advertising is a result of using all your marketing insights (and your brand positioning) to create an advertising message designed to appeal to your target market. The line between advertising and marketing is somewhat blurred. Broadly, advertising is any part of marketing where you pay to use someone else's other media channels to share your message. When you strategically bundle channels together to reach your target client market via several avenues simultaneously, this is an *advertising campaign*.

And now that you know the distinction between advertising and marketing, you can pedantically correct people whenever you like.

Make shouting about your services your number one priority!

Those who spend their careers producing advertising and marketing materials for others are often the worst at finding the time or motivation to execute their own marketing activities. So, when you start making concerted efforts to promote yourself, you are already putting yourself leaps and bounds ahead of people who are still "getting around to it." No business gets started—or maintains momentum and growth—without constant and consistent promotional activity.

The strategies you use to gain greater visibility than your competition and form better relationships with potential clients should be at the core of your marketing. Marilyn Heywood Paige, CMO of full-service agency Paige Black and an Adjunct Professor of Marketing, highlights to her students the importance of having a purpose and logic underlying every marketing effort,

> Strategy is not tactics. Tactics are things like video, social media, building websites, digital ads, SEO, etc. Strategic marketing is much more complex than you think, and it involves market research and a thorough situation analysis. If you are starting your work with tactics, you are not using a strategic approach.

Your approach to marketing strategy must remain flexible, what works one year may be entirely ineffective the next. Here are some of my observations on the various marketing and advertising activities we have pursued.

Paid local advertising

To quote John Wanamaker, a US department store merchant at the turn of the 20th century, "Half the money I spend on advertising is wasted; the trouble is, I don't know which half." Wanamaker's observation still largely holds true today. That said, effective promotional activities for solo-entrepreneurs and fledgling start-ups often require a greater investment of creativity, time, and effort than hard cash investment. Cash is *not* the key to effective marketing. Is it nice to have money to spend on marketing? Sure. Is it essential? Nope! Countless businesses have poured huge amounts of money into complex marketing strategies and multichannel advertising campaigns that have achieved very little. Reaching the right people, at the right time, with the right message trumps mere financial spend.

Prior to online advertising we would frequently run adverts and editorial in traditional paper media: The business supplements of the local press and regional trade publications. At the time every other local business advertised in a similar manner. So, we joined them. Paying for an ad in the local press went alongside being listed in the Yellow Pages (if you're under 30 years of age, you may need to Google that), everyone paid to be listed in directories simply because there really weren't many other options. Back in the day this type of advertising was relatively effective. Yet, the notion of placing an ad in the local press and bracing yourself for the phone to be ringing off the hook was—and remains—wishful thinking.

As online marketing became all-pervasive, we stopped booking press ads, and in return the local press and trade magazines ceased taking an interest in us editorially. We did not notice any adverse effects from ceasing to use print media. However, in the past couple of years we have resurrected (to a small degree) our use of the trade press and local editorial, largely because of their increased visibility online. We have been featured in editorial pieces about women in business, and we have contributed our expertise to charity events and subsequently been credited in the press coverage.

Again, I stress, we have still not attributed any paid work as a direct result of traditional press coverage. But as the local business community is more connected than ever before we have become more aware of the positive effect of exposure. Off the back of trade-press editorial, clients we have lost touch with might drop us a message on LinkedIn to catch up, and we get recognised at networking events by people already familiar with our business. While our ads or editorial are running, we will also crank up the heat on the quantity of our LinkedIn messages, and send warm-contact emails to people likely to have recently read the publication where we recently appeared. We will use an introduction such as "Hi, you may have seen us in today's issue of..."

Unless you are a major brand, placing ads across national media, simply buying an advert, and expecting work to come through the door is somewhat naïve. You need to be out there, in person, actively networking at the same time. Advertising can raise the visibility of your name and create an association with video production expertise, but it will not do the job on its own. If you choose to advertise (or try to get editorial coverage) in traditional media, be certain that the rest of your marketing strategy is also working hard to connect with that same audience via other means.

Chambers of Commerce

It is relatively inexpensive to become a member of your local Chambers of Commerce, and they often attract the right sort of members to be in the market for video production. Chambers of Commerce often hold networking events and business-to-business (B2B) trade exhibitions. I'm sure some businesspeople consider Chambers to be not quite as "cool" as independent networking get-togethers, but you get out what you put in, and regular attendance can open doors to credible clients in your local area. Our local Chamber has a very well-produced website and we frequently send them news stories for publication, our website's analytics show that we do get a few referrals to our website from them. So, check how switched-on they are when it comes to promoting your business online, and to other Chamber members.

You will likely find other local production companies are members, but do not be put off if a competitor is already a regular face. We have hosted exhibition stands at commerce shows, and fellow production companies have wandered over to talk shop. If nothing else, meeting fellow producers can be a useful intelligence-gathering exercise, or even a potential for collaboration. Remember, being a member of a Chamber does not by default operate as a promotional tool without some "leg work" by yourself. You need to use Chambers of Commerce to build your personal network.

Website

Yes, a website. You *do* still need a website. We have had a presence online in some form since the mid-1990s, and it remains a valuable showcase. Your site will be a central catchall place where all your promotional examples and expertise can be tied together in a style and order of your choosing. That said, as a consumer, I now tend to find businesses via their social media or LinkedIn. I then go to their website to find out more about their services or products. A website is part of a marketing funnel, and not a first-call destination in and of itself. Unlike social media, your own website is entirely under your control, and adaptable in any way you choose.

So, I would argue that your website doesn't have to be all things to all people, and it doesn't need to be overly complicated. You have two options: Outsource the build or do it yourself. I have already made the educated guess that you've got a creative streak.

The most successful sites we've had to date have been the ones we developed in-house with an off-the-peg Wordpress template that we packed with showreels, excellent photography, carefully written marketing copy, all designed to push a visitor toward a contact form. We also put in place a live chat feature enabled during office hours. The live chat was a complete shot in the dark, an inexpensive plugin we added to the site as an experiment. It turned into a high-converting contact method. The chat feature allowed visitors to pick our brains about a query without the feeling of commitment that can be associated with a phone call. It can also allow us to filter total non-starters, i.e. when the chat window pops up with the question "How much does a video cost?" we can say with a high degree of certainty that the conversation is unlikely to progress beyond this point.

There are some great pre-built portfolio sites that simply require the addition of examples of your work: Adobe's Behance, Squarespace, or the profile pages of freelance directory sites. Each has its benefits (simplicity and low, or no, cost) but as with social media, they are not under your ownership or control.

Having mentioned the upsides of building your own website, I would also caution against the DIY approach if you are not 100 % sure of your abilities (or your willingness to learning web development). Creating a website yourself can be a major time-suck, and the ongoing maintenance can become a frequent distraction. Yes, I have built several reasonable websites using inexpensive Wordpress themes, and there are thousands of YouTube tutorials to get newbies started. But, despite the positives (and the valuable learning experience), I have also spent countless hours trawling forums and requesting support tickets to find solutions to weird bugs that a professional developer could have rectified in a matter of seconds. The likelihood of coming unstuck grows exponentially if you also need to tailor your site's functions with plugins and search engine optimisation (SEO) considerations.

Our business has had many websites during the past 25 years, some of them created by solo-developers, while others were months in creation at big-name web design agencies. Do your homework and make sure whoever will be building your site really understands your business requirements. On occasions we have found designers and developers can really struggle when designing websites that must include lots of video and portfolio items. Showing off our diverse range of productions at their best while keeping page-load speeds swift has often been a headache.

Search marketing and design agencies might excel when tasked with the creation of an ecommerce or straightforward business presence website. They can throw a whole toolbox of tested techniques to get a site operational and indexed, then readily gather the analytics that demonstrate the effectiveness of their work. In our line of work there is not an "Add to basket" button to enable anyone to accurately pinpoint what is working and what is not, the process is much messier. The conversion of an enquiry into a paying client might take several weeks (or months) of communication outside of the website "funnel." Developers have, in my experience, come unstuck when creating a website to market bespoke creative solutions.

Google Ads

Make a search on Google—especially for any kind of commercial content—and the results at the top of the first page will be prefixed with "Ad."

From an advertiser's perspective Google Ads operates a somewhat mysterious bidding system. Getting your ad to the revered No.1 position on the front page of the results, and getting your intended audience to click on it is not simply a case of outbidding everyone else who is targeting their ad with the same search terms. In fact, it is possible to waste truly eye-watering amounts of cash on a scattergun campaign that tries to reach anyone and everyone. I am talking expenditure in the realms of tens of thousands a year.

So, how do you make Ads bring you paying business without costing the same as a human salary every month? Long story short, I *really* wish I knew the answer; I have long held conflicted feelings about Pay-Per-Click (PPC) campaigns.

For a while we administered PPC in-house to reasonably positive effect, but eventually the tinkering required to keep campaigns functioning at their optimum became a time-suck. We outsourced our search marketing to outside agencies. During the time we put the management of our account out of house we engaged no less than three different search marketing specialists. The fees associated with outsourcing were not inexpensive. Including clicks, the cost was sometimes four figures a month. Yet, even after three prolonged attempts, it stubbornly remained a major time-suck and burnt through more cash than it ever returned. Even with genuine "experts in the field" managing the campaigns, the income attributable to PPC was all but negated by the time and money invested in pursuing it.

Cold contact

The effectiveness of "cold contact" has been in question for years. The terrible reputation cold calling has earned itself will surely have put many people off picking up the phone to reach out for new business. Cold calling *can* work, but only with a lot of solid *strategy* and careful research driving it. You can waste hours—even weeks—calling random businesses to ask whether they might need video production services.

From decades of experience we know it is exceptionally unlikely to strike lucky and call someone at just the right moment. Our lead time from initial contact—through dozens more call, emails, LinkedIn messages, and trying to meet them in person at social events—can be a very protracted process. In the case of one client we won, the process of being given an opportunity to pitch for a project took 13 phone calls, and 10 emails over a period of almost 2 years.

The purpose of cold calling is not to beat people over the head with sales spiel, it is to introduce yourself, get an email address, ask if you can connect on LinkedIn, find out about their business needs, keep the contact warm and—to use an advertising term—"front of mind" until the day they do have a need for your skills. At that point they will pick up the phone to call you. A great deal of persistence and a lot of patience are key to making cold calling worthwhile in the longer-term.

It may be tempting to simply outsource your cold calling to someone who promises the earth or offers to work on commission. However, I would strongly advise against trying to use a third-party to develop personal relationships on your behalf. We have tried the outsourced approach. The providers were enthusiastic—promising returns beyond our wildest dreams—but they were not at all experienced in our line of work, and they were not able to convey our expertise or enthusiasm. They struggled to do any more than work through bulk lists of people who would either refuse the call or were adamant they would never have any interest in our services.

My take on this; *you* know *your business* and the benefits of your services far better than anyone else ever could. *You* are the person who should be calling new contacts and trying to form a relationship with them. As for getting shot down; if the people you call simply flat-out say they would have absolutely no use for your services it means you have not done your research properly. If they are unwilling to outsource, then it is pointless to keep pursuing them. If they do not have the money to outsource, again, scratch them from your contact list. Draw up logical lists of people to contact, i.e. those with a distinct need for video, and both the willingness and the ability to pay for it.

Draw up a schedule to do your calling and keep track of your efforts. As with all marketing and promotional activity you will not be able to accurately measure if the effort has been worthwhile unless you are recording your results. If you really cannot attribute any valuable leads to the activity, you can consider putting a stop to it. Initially you should concentrate your outreach efforts on a single business sector, ideally a sector where your showreel can demonstrate your relevant previous experience. When you get a glimmer of interest and a productive call, keep them high on your list and set a reminder to follow up later to check on any projects they may be considering.

LinkedIn

For many years I dismissed LinkedIn as a superficial network for stroking corporate egos. Undeniably, an element of its community does use it for little else except crowing about their achievements, or posting cryptic self-congratulatory comments accompanied by photos of champagne or a tropical beach. Do not be *that* person! However, recently I have gone full throttle with LinkedIn and the platform is beginning to pay dividends. The key to making LinkedIn work for you is to simply be helpful with no expectation of receiving anything in return. LinkedIn should be approached in the same way as real-life networking (plenty more on that later). Marilyn Heywood Paige suggests taking gradual steps toward an introduction,

> First, engage with the posts the target audience is putting out. Like, comment, and share the target's posts once or twice a week. Let them get to know you slowly over time. Tag them on posts you create that you think would be of genuine interest to them. Only after they have acknowledged your comments or posts should you send a direct message to them. It shouldn't be overly solicitous, just an invitation to connect, and perhaps have a networking Zoom call.

I have found LinkedIn to be most useful when used in combination with in-person networking. When someone has previously communicated with you in person, they are more likely to comment on, or share, your posts, thus amplifying your exposure, and adding their validation to what you are putting out on LinkedIn.

Social media, YouTube, and Vimeo

Do not fall prey to the misconception of inexperienced clients, believing that social media is a simple case of "build it and they will come." Everyone wants something they have produced to "go viral," but the internet does not work like that, especially in B2B promotion. Your videos should undoubtedly be eye-catching and professionally produced, but simply accumulating a showcase of your work on social media will likely achieve zilch. Corporate clients are not entirely without appreciation of the visual arts, but they will also view your showcase with a degree of cynicism, "Yeah, it *looks* good, but did it actually achieve what the client needed?"

Marilyn makes the point that every example of work you post on social media should be backed by the rationale behind its creation or—even better—the measurable result it produced for your client,

> Keep showing your work. Every day, release at least one clip *but* also explain what it *accomplishes*. Detail the problem the client was trying to solve and how this video solved it. Problems such as educating their customers, brand recognition, repositioning a product or value proposition, reputation management, recruiting new employees, building trust, etc. Corporations don't respond to just pretty films. They want to know you can solve problems for them and tell the story they need to tell effectively. Use hashtags in the post, and tag different contacts that you think would benefit from seeing the clip.

Marilyn's last recommendation is especially important. Think about which one of your prospective clients would like to see the piece of work you're posting and direct them to it, either with a mention or a friendly email with a link and a damn good reason why they should go watch. This is not to say that your social output must be dry and corporate. While your potential clients will be looking for proof of results, they will also want to see that you understand social media, especially if social is the final destination for the videos they may ask you to produce for them. Jarry Lee is an actress, model, and a content creator commissioned by major brands. At the time of writing, Jarry has more than 580,000 followers on Instagram.

> Many people feel uncomfortable about self-promotion, especially when done in a public way on social media. However, social media is such a powerful tool for self-marketing and 'level of comfort' really shouldn't get in the way! Content creators should learn to feel comfortable in taking pride in their work and showcasing it on social media. It can be helpful to think of it as a business strategy or as a free opportunity for exposure. It's also important to continue to engage with one's audience, and others in the same industry, to build a loyal and active community. I think developing a reputation as easy to work with is also important, but it can be more difficult to do on social media. At the end of the day, businesses seem to still weigh the 'fit' of a portfolio more heavily than someone's approachability or easiness to get along with. Showcasing a variety of commissioned work on social media can be helpful in demonstrating versatility. But if someone has worked with the same business

repeatedly, that work can show that they're reliable and good to work with. Engaging with other similar content creators or even businesses on YouTube could be helpful in creating a community. Anyone can upload a portfolio of their work to any video platform, but businesses love to see that a producer has an engaged audience and following.

In summary

- Understand the distinction between marketing and advertising, and the crossovers between the two. Not only will you be using both to promote your *own* business, but much of the work you produce for your clients will need to meet the goals of *their* marketing strategies.
- Marketing is everything you do to position your business so that it appeals to your ideal target clients. When it comes to marketing, your own creativity and personal effort usually trumps cash investment.
- Advertising is a part of marketing, and it is most often the part where you pay to use someone else's media channels to get your message out.
- Develop a good understanding of how advertising functions. A grasp of the world of advertising will be doubly beneficial for you. You will be better able to produce videos that function effectively for your clients, and you will also better understand how to promote yourself more effectively. I can highly recommend The Drum as a source of news and insights into the UK's marketing and advertising sector, https://www.thedrum.com.
- There are near-infinite and ever-changing ways to promote yourself. Give things a try, and if they do not work simply stop doing them. Remain sceptical but open-minded, try not to become cynical about trying new promotional strategies.
- If a newspaper or magazine gets in touch offering you a cut-price advert, but they need your commitment quickly, resist the temptation. Advertising requires well-planned strategy and careful execution; last-minute purchases bypass this important process. Do not let someone else derail your strategy.
- Do not use LinkedIn as a method of superficial self-congratulation. Be genuine, be helpful. Approach potential clients as you would in a real-world networking situation.
- Use social media strategically. Post examples of your work daily, with explanations of why they delivered exactly what the client requested. Be spontaneous and sociable but ensure most of your posts are made to serve a defined purpose.
- Unless you are an influencer with millions of fans feverishly waiting for everything you post, you are going to need to direct prospective clients toward posts that are potentially of interest to them. Your social media needs to tap into the contacts you have made in the real world.

7 Business networking

If you don't have a network, it's likely no one has heard of you!

Your production skills are only one aspect of why people choose to work with you; your reputation and personality are usually what gets you in front of people who might want to work with you. Whenever we hear of a new competitor in the business, it is rarely because of their marketing or advertising; it is because new entrants to the market are relentlessly self-promoting. They make themselves highly prolific. Whether it is a networking event, an art exhibition, a film festival, or a charity event, they will attend and will be the life and soul of the party. They will crop up in business conversations frequently, "Oh yeah, I met them last week. They seem to be everywhere right now." The best thing about self-promotion is that marketing *yourself* costs next to nothing yet is *highly effective*. I have observed that once a competitor has gained traction in their new business, and has got some clients on board, their self-promotional efforts become less regular. They cease to be a "new face" on the scene, and begin to blend in. So, that is your competitive edge. Even when your business is running at full capacity, make sure you are still prolific. Be everywhere, talk to anyone who will listen. When you are busy it can be tempting to ease off the gas, or maybe outsource promotional activity to someone else. Remember, you founded the business. No one else can uniquely represent your business the way that you can! It is a great sense of achievement to show up to an event and be able to talk from the heart about the business you created.

No doubt most entrepreneurs will insist that networking is the only true way to find new clients: "it's not what you know, but who you know," and "All the real business gets done on the golf course" and so forth. There is a great deal of truth in those sayings. Those who gain the greatest results from professional networking take a highly strategic and selective approach to the time they spend meeting and greeting. They also actively work on continually improving their networking, developing their interpersonal skills, and emulating the most charismatic networkers.

Without clients you do not have a production company. If you are not earning money from paying clients, you are quite simply making videos as a hobby. Clients make a business. Yet, creatives are often uncomfortable "selling" their talent. Initially, I really disliked networking. I did not understand the point of it, and I could never get my head around disparate businesspeople getting together to make small talk. I just had a nagging feeling there were better ways to be spending my time. However, I have—over the course of several years—forced myself to try a smorgasbord of networking events, trade shows, masterminds, and business-breakfasts aimed at all tiers of the corporate community.

Yes, I concede the truth that you only need to be lucky once to meet the big fish who becomes your next major client. It is certainly true that if you can attend networking events of the very highest calibre, a few introductions to the "right people" can reward you with regular work for years to come. To meet those perfect matches, you will have to invest countless hours of your own time making certain you are seen everywhere. Networking events are often held out of business hours, or at "stupid-o-clock" in the morning. Nine times out of ten you will spend an hour trying to awkwardly detach yourself from stilted conversations with consultants, estate agents, and people looking for their next job. The wine is often rather unpleasant too. Hey, maybe I just gripe too much? Enough with the cynicism.

Although networking events can be hit-or-miss, I rarely turn down the opportunity to try a new one. Almost all networking groups offer a free ride for potential new members. You will almost certainly get a feel for the professionalism of the organiser from the outset. It is easy to spot when your time is being wasted. I spoke to Fiona Duncan-Steer, a UK-based Writer and Business Coach, and Founder of the RSViP Business Networking Agency. Fiona offered an insight into how modern networking events are (or at least, should be) organised,

> So many events get this wrong, with their overly-structured and mundane formats and this is what led me to launch the events I have successfully ran for over ten years now. By introducing a strong social element into an event, you are immediately providing an experience which is not only useful and productive, but enjoyable. Isn't it better to look forward to attending a networking event, as opposed to dreading it? There is no secret formula for a successful networking event, it's a whole host of aspects cleverly pulled together to create the final piece, however if you do anything, at least make your guests smile.

First, where is the event held?

I can tell a lot about the likely quality of networking by the venue alone. Almost every "informal networking" evening (with the emphasis on *informal*) that I have attended at a bar or pub has been a mess. If you cannot identify who is there to network, and who has just come along for a drink, it is a surefire waste of time. On the other hand, "socials" with a guestlist of people in a similar business to your own, or events that are based around a common theme, or a guest speaker, can be useful for staying in the loop on what's happening on the local grapevine; if you want to know who has lost what client and under what circumstances, a few beers can loosen the tongues of all the right people.

All the "business-breakfasts" I have attended comprised of sleepy people moaning about the quality of the buffet, followed by a mass exodus to the car park to get to the office before rush hour. Anyone who is truly a "morning person" is already at either the gym or the office when the business-breakfast crowd are assembling. I happily pass on the opportunity to attend any of them.

Second, does the host do some matchmaking?

Is the event's organiser proactive in fostering potential working relationships? The most professional networking events I have attended screen wannabe members beforehand; they made the effort to meet with me a few days in advance to understand how they could make the event worthwhile for me. They took the time to ask who I was hoping to talk with, and on my arrival, they made some introductions to get the ball rolling.

At the very worst networking event I attended, the organiser simply pointed me out and yelled to the room that someone new was "giving it a try" and announcing that I "film stuff for people." Despite sending them an email ahead of time with a short bio of myself and the business, they still handed me a badge with both my name and that of the business spelled incorrectly. The quality of the welcome often sets the tone for the rest of the event, so ask whether the host is actively matchmaking and performing introductions.

Third, is it just a regular clique of the same of faces?

If your first impressions of an event have been positive, make sure you attend a second before committing to any kind of membership or regular payment. So far, no networking group has refused me another free ticket to help me reach a decision. Also, keep a watch on whether an event continues to be valuable to you. I have been a member of a couple of paid networking groups whose guest speakers became progressively more lacklustre, and an event calendar that began to dwindle. If a group has lost its energy, cancel the membership fee.

A few years ago, I tried an evening of "speed networking" in a hotel bar. On each table was a timer, and each guest was allowed two minutes to tell the person opposite about themselves and their services. It was a novelty, and I continued conversation with a couple of reasonably credible businesspeople over the canapés that followed. I was intrigued-enough to attend the following month's event, having negotiated another invite as a freebie. On the night, the very same guests from the first event drifted in, and the host seated us at the same tables, we circulated the room in the same order, and undertook roughly the same two-minute pitch to each other under a strange pretence that we'd not met before. Several times I overheard, "It's okay, I think I've already got some of your cards." I chalked the peculiar evening up to strange fluke and paid to attend a third event. For a third time I met the exact same people, and the strange charade of well-rehearsed elevator pitches to the same regular drinking-buddies happened once again!

Many networking groups reveal themselves to be quite stale after only the first or second visit. If you are the only new member in attendance—and at the next event there are no other new faces to talk to—it is most likely a local business clique posing as a networking event. If you are not being proactively introduced to people to discuss professional topics, it's most likely just a social mixer.

Lastly, would any of the attendees give you work?

The foremost question I ask myself before accepting any invitation is "Are there going to be potential clients I can talk to?" Often—if I am being pragmatic—I can turn down an invite with complete confidence I am not going to be missing out. Sure, there are degrees of separation, with the outside chance of a referral to someone outside the immediate group; but by and large if the type of people you're trying to reach are not going to be there, attending will be pointless.

The golden rule of networking events: You do not have to work the whole room and make small talk with everyone. People who desperately tour the room dishing out handfuls of cards to everyone in sight are not there to develop mutually beneficial relationships. Developing just a single new and genuine relationship that you can follow up afterwards is worth more than a fistful of "I know neither of us will actually bother to stay in touch" business cards. I often wait for a few days after the event before I get in touch. No one is going to give me much more than a "Yeah, nice to meet you too" response if I ping them an email the moment I leave the event. Your new contact will be inundated with messages quickly fired out by other attendees. Give it a few days, then follow up with something more sincere than a "Nice to meet you" pleasantry.

Run your own event

Using tools such as Eventbrite and Meetup, it's easier than ever to create and operate your own business networking event: Be it a regular get together of businesses in your immediate area, or a less frequent learning event to explain your service offering while answering common questions or dispelling myths about video production. Your event must offer additional value to guests, not merely be a sales pitch. We have run a successful biannual event, co-hosted with a media agency and a broadcaster, to "recruit" new clients. The half-day event—with catering—can attract potential clients from further afield. You will need to invite a *lot* of people to your event. Typically, there is a very high dropout rate as the date of the event approaches, and naturally there will also be a lot of no-shows on the day. We usually lose 50% of confirmed attendees somewhere along the way. That said, the ones who do make the effort to attend have a genuine interest in discussing a business need or a potential production with us after the event—hence the wine and canapés!

You do not have to go to the extent of operating a full-scale networking event. Instead, you could invite a few "movers and shakers" on the local business scene to a monthly dinner at a good restaurant. This is often called a "mastermind"; it is an opportunity to talk business in an off-the-record manner.

Networking can take many forms; the only objective is to achieve genuine and meaningful conversations with the right people. The right people can *even* include your competitors.

Networking with fellow producers

It is natural to feel, to some degree, that "competitors" are unwelcome intruders, trying to steal work off your plate—especially if a small pool of producers in a city are frequently vying for the attention of the same clients. This makes me think of the way young schoolchildren hug their arms around their exercise books while they write—hiding their work out of sight—fearing the other kids are going to copy them.

Yes, it might seem counterintuitive to foster friendly professional networks with people from other production companies. Yet, your competitors (imagine the word contained in air quotes) can often be a potential source of work and mutual support. Production companies do not often attempt to be all things to all people; every business will have strengths and weaknesses—and it just might be that your competitor's next project requires one of *your* business' strongest talents.

For example, my production company has its own high-specification sound studio. Top-end microphones and carefully designed acoustic dampening is not a facility that other nearby producers could justify constructing for infrequent use—so, we regularly take bookings from other production companies needing to record dialogue or mix soundtracks. On the flipside, when a potential client recently approached us to livestream a product launch, we happily passed the brief on to a contact with far more experience than ourselves in the staging and streaming of large corporate events. Practising "good karma" when networking with fellow professionals can lead to valuable referrals and collaborative projects.

How to be a great networker

If you are still not quite at ease with the prospect of networking, I feel your discomfort. I used to be far from confident, the mere thought of wandering up to strangers at a business gathering and starting a conversation would freak me out. I mentioned this to Fiona of RSViP Business Network, and as a well-practised serial networker, Fiona offered this advice,

> Plan, prepare and relax. 'Plan' because then at least you help eliminate any nerves you may have when you walk into that busy room, at least you have a target of who you'd like to meet; for example, if you have requested the attendees list, have a scan down and create your wish list of who you are going to make a bee-line to talk to. This will ensure that you have a focus, which in turn will result in it being productive once those conversations have taken place. 'Prepare'. This is similar to 'Plan' in that practically you can earmark a few names from the guest list that you plan to chat to, however preparation also falls on you personally to ensure that you are creating the right first impression in the room, after all first impressions count. So, what can you do? Choose your outfit carefully, is it professional attire? Does it reflect your personality and your brand? Ensure you are presentable, it may sound like common sense, but you'd be surprised how many people I meet who look unkempt, unironed clothes, dirty shoes, etc. Remember you are a window into your brand so be aspirational. Mental preparation is also key when attending networking events. Make sure you are open to it, in a good mood and feeling on top form. If you don't feel your best self then perhaps give it a wide berth on that occasion, it could do you more harm than good and give an inaccurate impression of your true self just because you are having an off day.

I can especially associate with Fiona on her final point; I recall an event I had signed up for weeks in advance, a "quiz night" for local businesses. I am not a fan of such events as they do not usually draw senior decision-makers, and networking is not really on the agenda. Nonetheless, a new client had extended the invite and I agreed to go. I was having problems with a home renovation I was managing at the time, plus I had a fraught day at the office, and as I made my way to the event the weather turned bad. I wanted nothing more than to turn back and head home. The quiz turned out to be terribly organised and poorly attended. I was getting frustrated and began clock-watching. I chose to make my apologies and leave before the quiz was over. I probably looked like an ass for walking out, but it was my own fault. I began having pangs of regret the moment I had agreed to attend. Even the most sparkling conversation partner would have struggled to find anything pleasant about being in my company that night. Since that crappy evening I kept in mind that if my reaction to an invite isn't an immediate "Hell yeah, sign me up now!" then it should almost certainly be a "Thanks but no thanks." Fiona concludes,

> Finally 'Relax'. Don't take it too seriously—it's only a networking event—be yourself, people will see right through you if you are being

> ingenuine. If you don't relax while there, it will show. Nerves is an obvious one, so do whatever you need to do to prepare yourself and get into the zone to ensure you are the best version of yourself. People are often drawn to confidence, so if you exude this it will reflect your brand in a positive light. People will naturally want to know more about you.

I am inclined to be an introvert by nature; being relaxed and making small talk has often felt rather superficial and difficult to initiate. But I have also nurtured a lifelong interest in personal development. It became clear that my clumsy half-assed approach to social niceties was holding me back. "Small talk" is the oil that gets social cogs turning, it is far from superficial. Most importantly, I have now come to rather dislike people who skip the small talk and just hit me with a business card and a rehearsed elevator pitch. I am treated to an entire verbal brochure of their business offering before I have even had time to memorise their name. So, I made a resolution to learn how to do small talk well. Fiona also cautions networkers to steer clear of rehearsed and "salesy" opening gambits,

> Don't sell to anyone full stop. You are not there to do that, you are there to make new connections, strengthen existing ones, and build relationships. Just by having conversations with someone you are already selling yourself, your personality, and your 'why'. If they like you, they will buy from you, refer you, and support you. So, don't attend with the intention of selling your services; this approach is wrong, wrong, wrong! You can, however, be sure to tell people about your services in the conversations you are having, share success stories, case studies, perhaps you have done something you are really proud of recently, this will intrigue and lead to questions naturally, without you having to 'sell' anything. Nobody likes a smart ass; be confident in yourself and your business while careful not to cross over into the realms of arrogance. You can show this in how you carry yourself, your body language, your conversational and social skills and your handshake for example, make it strong, make eye contact with people, smile, ask questions, avoid talking about yourself too much and wait for people to ask you. Make sure you know how to explain what you do in a clear, concise way. Be a storyteller: nobody cares *what* you do, they care *why* you do it.

If you would like to know more about Fiona, you can visit her personal website, www.fionaduncansteer.co.uk, and to see how a legitimate professional networking group presents itself online go check out www.rsvipnetwork.co.uk.

I endlessly scour the internet for business insight. Many business blogs and podcasts were often short-lived marketing exercises, so I was not keen to reference them in the book. However, several of my most rewarding sources of learning have stayed the course and are kept fresh daily. These resources stand head and shoulders above anything else I found out there; so, I will happily wait here while you go and check them out:

How to sell your services without being sleazy: Ramit Sethi—*I Will Teach You to Be Rich*

Ramit Sethi is a unique entrepreneur who sits at the intersection of business, personal finance, and psychology. I urge you to sign-up to all Ramit's newsletters and devour everything he publishes. Sethi provides a masterclass of entertaining, honest, and refreshing business communications. I also appreciate the production quality of Ramit's videos, they are textbook examples of video marketing and training done just right. As a bonus, you will also learn a tremendous amount of valuable information to help you manage your finances.

www.iwillteachyoutoberich.com

How to network without being a bore: "Charisma on Command"—YouTube channel

If you've ever wanted to know how to become the most engaging and charismatic person in the room, you'll find the 'Charisma on Command' channel an Aladdin's cave of well-produced videos that will tutor you to handle any social situation with energy and panache.

www.youtube.com/user/charismaoncommand

Insights into the mindsets of the world's top performers: Tim Ferriss—"The Tim Ferriss Show"

Tim Ferriss is an American entrepreneur, start-up investor, and the author of several global best-selling books. Tim is also the host of a tremendously insightful podcast. Not only is Tim a fascinating guy to listen to, he also discusses how to communicate with people at the very top of their game.

https://tim.blog/

For frank and honest insights into the future of marketing: Gary Vaynerchuk—"Vaynermedia"

I am confident there is no one working in advertising or marketing who does not know of the mighty 'Gary Vee'. If not, you are missing out. He provides a flow of frank, no-BS insights into current and future marketing trends. For Gary, relevance, sincerity, and immediacy far outweigh production values. His language is, er... 'passionate'. You will either love or hate the guy, but everything comes from the heart and with great candor. He is prolific across all social media, but 'The Gary Vee Audio Experience' is my go-to podcast for uplifting life and business advice.

www.garyvaynerchuk.com

Implement a Customer Relationship Management system

To wrap up this chapter, I want to highlight the importance of keeping track of your new contacts and potential clients, the progress being made in your marketing activities, and the ongoing contact you have with your existing clients. Your marketing efforts should never be sporadic. If it is not planned and scheduled, it likely will not get done! To be effective, your marketing must have clear objectives directed by careful planning.

Keeping records of your marketing and networking activity helps you not only figure out what's working and what's not, it also provides a means to be automatically reminded to chase contacts and revisit opportunities that have gone cold. We have all met someone and told them to stay in touch as we may have a need for their services, only to never hear from them again. Even making the effort to chase someone a second time and getting a firm "no thanks" ensures no one falls through the cracks. We have plenty of clients who were followed-up every five or six months for several years until converting into a billable project. So, until you get a firm no—or deduce there is no chance of work—regularly stay in touch with everyone you add to your contact book.

We maintain all our marketing data in a cloud-based CRM (Customer Relationship Management) system. There is a myriad of CRM options available. We use an account with Hubspot; but Insightly, Salesforce, and Zoho are all respected services that have been operational for several years. All of them can cater for users from individuals to organisations with thousands of employees.

Every CRM platform will provide you with a detailed contact book, a place to store notes about your dealings with current clients, your research, and the history of your contact with potential clients. There will also be a calendar system, providing the ability to set prompts to call or email those prospective clients later.

We used to keep track of our marketing efforts in an Excel sheet—feeling that simplicity was the surefire way to stay on track—but once we began using a CRM system our marketing began to operate far more smoothly. As a small venture starting out, several CRM platforms will be free of charge, and it would be remiss not to get your customer relationship and marketing operations in order from day one.

In summary

- The busiest and most affluent businesspeople are not necessarily the most talented in their industry. Often, they are just very comfortable networkers. They get good at being high profile and making sure they put themselves "in the right place at the right time."
- Networking, at its most simple, is just getting to know new people and finding out how you can help each other. Networking does not have to

be an organised group event, it can simply be taking someone for lunch. Meeting the *right* people is more important than meeting a lot of people.

- Show humility and enthusiasm. Take a genuine interest in chatting to others and getting to know about their businesses. If you meet a competitor at an event, follow the same advice—your business could well be the missing piece in their puzzle (or vice versa).
- You will very rarely leave any networking event with the promise of work, that is not the way it plays out.
- Take a strategic approach to finding events to attend and people to meet. The best networkers put in the research and hours necessary to mix in the right circles.
- Networking isn't "cheating." It is very difficult for *any* business to gain traction—and find new opportunities—if its owner isn't consistently making the effort to get to know new people.
- Try to attend every networking event you can, but do not feel obligated to attend again, or even to stick around to the end. If you immediately have a gut-feeling that the event is not right for you, or that you are unlikely to connect with the right people, it is okay to make a graceful and polite exit.
- If you are interested in attending regularly and there is a ticket price or membership fee, ask to attend a second event for free before agreeing to a regular commitment.
- Formal events with a published guestlist, a theme for discussion, or an invited speaker often attract the right kind of attendees. Formal events are also more likely to do introductions and matchmaking with people you might not otherwise meet.
- Casual social events can be good for hearing gossip about what is going on locally, and to talk shop in an "off-the-record" manner with other businesses; but they're often cliques that attract "regular faces" rather than prospective clients.
- Business-breakfasts are all types of wrong. Chatting with people awkwardly eating breakfast while trying not to get fried egg on their business attire is not for me. If you are a morning person, give them a shot. But do not feel bad if you prefer to network later in the day.
- If you get a whiff of "speed networking" or enforced "fun" activities, run for the hills! Serious businesspeople have better things to be doing. These are not the type of events that attract people likely to open new doors for you.
- If you really cannot find any event worth attending, consider creating your own. It doesn't need to be a group event; a low-key dinner with the right people will be more valuable than a room of a hundred people with no need of your skills.
- Take pride in being the type of person who can go to a networking event, on your own terms, to represent your own business, and make

meaningful conversation about a subject where you possess a unique talent. Many people struggle to feel at ease doing this, and they unknowingly miss out on great opportunities.

- You should accurately record the details of the new contacts you make into your CRM. For each of your contacts you should also note your follow-up communication and set reminders to prompt you to get back in touch at regular intervals.

8 The gig economy

Many of the traditional methods of promotion covered in the previous chapter rely on continual "maintenance" to keep your business at the front of potential clients' minds. You maintain continual effort to keep your exposure high, prompting and reminding potential clients of your existence, until they eventually want to commission something.

Many of the traditional methods are limited by geographic boundaries. Local press coverage or ads in trade magazines—even when they have an online presence—are unlikely to make an impact beyond an audience within a tight radius of your business. The same is true of in-person networking events. Yet, video production is—by and large—a service that you can offer in some form to clients all around the world. And right now, it is a buyer's market. A business can post a creative brief online, and within hours dozens of potential producers will have made introductions.

So, you can of course make a decent living by marketing your production business within your immediate region, but hey, the rest of the world is also available to do business. If you are already considering running your business from a coworking space, or entirely remotely, then you might already be a step ahead of me here! The "Gig Economy," fuelled by freelancers and collectives of remote workers, has provided you access to infinite opportunity without geographic boundaries.

Anyone, anywhere on the planet, wanting to commission a video production can fire their requirements out onto the internet. They just want a creative solution to their brief, whether they were aware of your business prior to receiving your pitch is not relevant.

So, today you not only have to operate a localised marketing strategy to maintain a continually high profile in your area, you also need to dedicate time to trawling the internet for open project briefs from further afield. If traditional marketing is a marathon, the gig economy is a sprint. You will need to work at a lightning-fast pace to locate, pitch for, and (hopefully) win highly competitive open briefs. So, where can you find all these paying gigs that require no marketing effort on your part?

Freelancing websites

There has been a rapid proliferation of freelance gig websites. Anyone with half an idea for a project can throw their scrappy thoughts into the world and wait for freelancers and small creative shops to place bids on bringing them to fruition.

I err on the side of caution with any type of competitive bidding where the emphasis is on going in with the lowest-cost estimate. I am in no doubt there are many decent opportunities to be had on these kinds of sites, on the proviso that you set yourself some ground rules and figure out what you are getting yourself into. Sort the wheat from the chaff and stick to a rigid set of criteria when screening the suitability of potential clients. If you get a gut-feeling that something about the project—or the individual who placed the brief—does not quite stack up, you are most likely correct. I have come to the personal belief that maybe 90% of the requests for bids on freelancing sites come from people who:

1 Are wholly unable to explain their project clearly, or even vaguely outline what they want to achieve. These people do not require your input on their brief, because they do not even know themselves what they are trying to do.
2 Caveat their requirements with a string of *"and more..."* or *"etc..."* Open-ended briefs, from wherever they originate, result in projects that spiral out of control, struggle to get signed off, or have the client perpetually believing they are owed more work from you.
3 Are offering ridiculously unfeasible budgets or hourly rates. Yet, you will often find dozens of creatives bidding for a tiny project, and they will often go in far below the already meagre amount of money offered by the listing. Also, beware of foreign currency conversions. Sometimes the exchange rate between currencies, minus the site's commission, minus PayPal fees, can reduce a small amount to just loose change.
4 Are tyre-kickers wondering how much a video might cost without a genuine commitment to progressing with the project. These people are just intrigued to receive some responses without being especially committed to commissioning anyone. Unfortunately, these sites can be open to abuse by people hoping creatives will send them a few free ideas, and for some reason they do!

How to sharpen a vague brief

I cannot stress the importance of gathering and understanding every detail of what the client is asking you to do. A clear brief is essential, whether the brief is a £500 project on a freelancing site or a £50,000 commission from a creative agency; the headaches caused by working to a vague brief will be just the same.

A thorough, detailed, brief is the foundation you will build days, weeks, or even months of work on top of. If the brief is vague, you must ask for clarification on every aspect that is not entirely clear. Never make assumptions. If clarification is not forthcoming, or the reply is still too vague to act on, you must let the client know that you cannot begin work on the project. If the brief is nebulous and lacking in specifics, it has the potential to grow into a monster. Ask for it to be refined until you have clear objectives and end points. If you begin a project without having clarified objectives and boundaries from the outset, you will do the work with an uneasy feeling that the job is never going to end, and that you are being taken advantage of. Every amendment the client wishes to make will cause you to further resent having taken on the project.

Resentment is not only an unpleasant feeling to carry throughout a project, it can also breed cynicism. You can inadvertently develop feelings that all clients are a nightmare, that you are a pushover, or that you are a player at the bottom end of the market. Have principles and try to stick to them. Set yourself a minimum acceptable fee, and never submit a bid for anything less. In a downward bidding war, the winner is often the worse-off for doing so; they are going to wind up being underpaid by someone who doesn't value their work and is probably going to keep cracking the whip in future.

Overall, I am not a big fan of freelancing sites, especially if you are trying to build a business that can maintain a reliable level of return business from corporate clients with ongoing video requirements. Freelancing sites seem to attract the worst type of potential clients, "done fast, done cheap." Granted, I am in no doubt there is good work to be found on these sites, and some of their members seem to have completed many projects, but I suspect they carefully screen the clients and the briefs that they take on. Have some pride, it is a sensible defensive strategy to set yourself firm criteria for when you should leave an "opportunity" for someone else to pursue.

Getting your client to the table

We have always preferred to nurture relationships with clients we can meet in person or at least via a phone call, Zoom, or Microsoft Teams. A closer relationship makes honest and positive conversations much easier, e.g. if the specified budget just is not realistic for the project they have in mind, we can manage expectations and discuss other options. We can consider what can best be achieved for their budget and help them modify the brief. Alternately we can help them understand why more investment may be necessary to achieve their goals. Such frank discussions can be difficult, or ultimately futile, when dealing with a client at arm's-length via email or messages relayed via a third-party. Unfortunately, freelancing websites can attract "hands off" clients who are outsourcing projects primarily because they *want* to maintain minimal contact. Always try to remain in frequent contact throughout a project; even if it is not always reciprocated, never go quiet on a client.

Pitch aggregation sites

Of course, the owners of an entrepreneurial production business must explore every online avenue in search of work. So, having outlined the pros and cons (admittedly, mostly cons) of lower-tier freelancing websites, let us move on to the higher-echelons of pitch aggregation websites. These pitching websites are beginning to proliferate, so keep searching for new entrants to the market.

Just as in business networking, there are the lower-tier gossip shops where businesspeople gather for drinks. Then there are more prestigious circles where businesspeople go to get real business done. Pitching sites such as Genero.com, and TheSmalls.com work on the same core principles as freelancing sites, except they specialise in advertising and corporate filmmaking projects. They act as middlemen between potential clients and film production companies and solo filmmakers. These sites require commissioning clients provide much fuller briefs to weed out speculative tyre-kickers, and they take a commission from the production budget. But, from the get-go *real* sums of money are in play, and that attracts genuine clients who want the job done right. The budgets on offer for most projects are usually realistic, and many of the clients are sometimes recognisable brand names and agencies.

One of the larger pitching sites, Genero, boasts a vast community of talented filmmakers all around the world. So, there is a serious amount of competition vying for the projects. But, as with the lottery, *someone* out there must win! Potential clients now flock to these aggregation sites; after all, why organise a string of meetings to brief a tiny handful of nearby producers when the entire world can be invited to pitch?

We pursued opportunities on these higher-tier pitching sites for a long time (a *very* long time) before our efforts eventually paid off. We won a commission for a series of social media videos for a major retail brand, a business we would have struggled to penetrate with our own marketing efforts. The gates were only opened to us when they requested an online "beauty parade" of potential new creators. The commission by the retailer was added to our Genero profile, and this "vote of confidence" by a recognisable brand seemed to solidify our position as a credible contender. The win-loss ratio of our pitches started to swing in the right direction. We had always put 100% effort into each pitch, they were all good submissions, but our eventual wins were only achieved through sheer bloody-minded persistence. Every loss was greeted with a "Right, let's move right onto the next one" attitude. When it comes to this en masse pitching scenario simply staying the course counts for a lot.

Naturally, the more recognisable a brand name is, the greater the number of agencies and production companies are going to be throwing their hats into the ring. This means the quality of pitches being submitted (at least by the folks with any chance of being shortlisted) will be exceptionally high. For the size of commissions we strive to win, we'll typically spend upwards of a week developing our creative approach, drafting the copy, and designing the pitch document. Often, we will produce demo work to accompany our pitch. It is a major investment of time—and it benefits greatly from being a team project—but such effort is required to be on the same stage as global competitors. You have got to pick your battles wisely, but the wins can be far more substantial.

But... there is a catch. Did you see that coming?

Well, a "catch" is a little harsh, it is a trade-off in return for receiving only filtered and qualified briefs. Pitching for work via aggregation sites puts a third-party between yourself and the prospective client. Any queries you may have about the project can usually only be relayed to the client via a gatekeeper, and that means you'll inevitably have to make some assumptions in your pitch (although questions you have about a brief can usually be forwarded to the client). The briefs on professional pitching sites are usually well-written with plenty of details, but at some stage in your pitch you are just going to have to take a shot in the dark and clarify the details further, if or when you get commissioned.

In summary

- The gig economy has broken down the barriers to finding amazing new clients all around the world. Projects are posted in plain sight, just waiting for you to pitch for the work. At the top tier of creative commissioning platforms, major national and global brands often post open briefs that—in the near past—only top-end agencies would have been granted the opportunity to look at.
- Syndicated open briefs are extremely competitive. In a traditional scenario, a business would do some research into production companies that might suit their needs, then invite just a handful of them to develop creative ideas and cost estimates. In an open briefing, the floodgates are opened!
- Clients posting open briefs have done so in the hope they will get an influx of great creative solutions. They do not want to be continually answering queries on their brief, which is why the pitching platform acts as a gatekeeper. So, unless it is a critical question that will affect your ability to pitch, you will have to make some assumptions. Try to anticipate every question the end client might ask of you and include the answers in your pitch.
- On the downside, the gig economy has created a free platform for nightmarish clients with delusional demands and little money to waste even *more* people's time. You deserve better. When scanning through sites for open briefs you need to be super-critical and read between the lines. If something does not feel right, it probably isn't.
- Avoid vague briefs. If a client cannot be bothered to formulate and clearly convey the outcomes they are hoping to achieve, it is unlikely you'll be

able to create work to adequately achieve those objectives. You'll be trying to hit a moving target.

- If you choose to give a brief that is lacking in detail the benefit of the doubt, ask for the project's requirements to be clarified. If the potential client still has ambiguous objectives, or leaves too many questions unanswered, they are setting you up for failure. This remains true no matter how much money is on offer.
- Always be wary of briefs that lack boundaries, make sure to agree a firm list of deliverables and due dates. Having defined outcomes will create boundaries and prevent the project scaling out of control.
- Be extra-vigilant about maintaining frequent and clear communication at all stages of the process. Keep in mind that when doing work via gig platforms, you will often be discussing subjective and nuanced creative matters with someone whose native language might not be English.
- If you intend to bid on a project in a foreign country, make sure to check the currency of the project. Is the budget still feasible after factoring in exchange rates, any commission due to the intermediary website, and fees by platforms such as PayPal?
- Set yourself high standards. You are talented, and you should work with clients who will value the work you do for them. Projects are being posted online around the clock, so if you have doubts about putting yourself forward for a project that you do not feel entirely confident about, don't. That's absolutely fine.

9 Public sector tenders

Why have I given an entire chapter to the subject of public sector tenders? Aren't the many online tender platforms just another offshoot of the gig economy? No. Public sector tenders are an entirely different beast. Now, I do not wish to portray the public sector as a bland collective of dull bureaucrats: People who get a small flutter of enjoyment from calling lengthy meetings about the cost of paperclips, *but* there is an *element* of truth. Your proposals will have to meet many criteria, and most of them will not be related to your creativity.

Private businesses, and even Public Limited Companies (PLCs), can largely spend their cash however they see fit. If they take a risk on pursuing a cool and edgy video project, they only need to defend that expense within their own walls. No doubt those in the public sector would love such freedoms, but they are spending taxpayers' money. Their expenditure is under frequent scrutiny and spending must be justified at many levels, sometimes publicly.

Public sector clients share the same objectives as private clients—they still want to commission high-quality video production—but they also need to work with a production company that has an appreciation of the type of hurdles they will have to clear at all stages of the process. Tenders are designed to weed out suppliers who would likely find it difficult to operate with the additional scrutiny and reporting requirements.

- Before you get demotivated, I should point out that not every public sector project gets hidden behind the firewall of a lengthy online tender process. You can still reach out *directly* to public sector departments to get the lay of the land, and even find video production projects being commissioned on a direct basis. These could be projects for non-profits, public healthcare, emergency services, the military, local authorities, universities, and colleges. For projects with a budget below set financial thresholds (you will be able to find current procurement regulations online) many regional and city-level departments can—and actively seek to—commission local small businesses without having to conduct a formal tender process. Instead of requesting tender applications they will conduct some form of "best-value exercise"—basically they will trawl around for a handful of comparable estimates to give them a paper trail that proves they sought competitive prices, and this is still how we find the majority of our public sector projects.

The exact requirements and regulations surrounding public sector work will differ by country, but most governments will operate some type of central procurement website with links to the tender portals in various specialisms, departments, or regions. It's usually possible to subscribe to email updates. In the UK, you can view live public contracts at www.gov.uk/contracts-finder and (at the time of writing) the US equivalent can be found at https://beta.sam.gov. That said, public sector contracts get disseminated across *hundreds* of portals (and you can spend a very significant amount of time trawling for opportunities) so you'll need to be quite specific in your criteria. You might want to Google terms such as "creative tenders," "video production tenders," or "videographer tenders."

Whether you are embarking on a public sector application via a formal procedure, or are in direct contact with a public department, you will undoubtedly have to meet criteria that many private sector clients couldn't care less about:

- You must demonstrate the actual steps of *how* you are going to complete the project, and do so in more explicit detail than would usually be of interest to a private client. When your tender is evaluated the recipient needs to see that you understand the importance of procedures, timelines, and the mitigation of potential risks—i.e. giving them confidence in your ability to smoothly *deliver* the production you are proposing.
- Even if the price of the commission is fixed, you still need to explain *why* you are competitive—demonstrate that you're a lean business that keeps costs under control, and is always looking for savings to get its clients more for their money.
- You should (if the tender allows) include case studies of comparable projects, demonstrating *how* they were delivered, and the feedback from those clients. A case study should give a sense of the size of your previous commissions, and the methodologies of *how* the projects were produced.

When working with a client in the public sector, it is essential to maintain frequent contact—people come and go. Following a job well-done you may be told that you have gained a place on a *recommended supplier* list. Great news! But I always remain a little sceptical (as you might have gathered). I imagine the mystical *recommended supplier* list to be just a Post-it stuck to someone's monitor. I'm sure it's something *far* more sophisticated (probably). Regardless, it helps to think of your "approved" status as lacking any real permanence. In several sectors it is mandatory to review supplier contracts at regular intervals, just to make sure no one has got too comfortable taking the money for contractual obligations that might be better served by another provider. Formal policies aside, you can gradually become distanced from the organisation that you jumped through a thousand hoops to get whitelisted by. You are often just one resignation or relocation at the client's end from being forgotten. The relationships you form require frequent nudges and reminders to be kept alive. Stay in touch, and keep abreast of where your contacts are, and where they are heading next. Whenever you hear of a change at the client's end introduce yourself to the recruit and get them up to speed on all the amazing work you completed for their predecessor.

Here is something important to remember; a healthy relationship with a client in the public sector depends on two factors. First, they get a return on the investment they made in your productions. They will be looking for either a financial return or some other measurable metric that matters to them; for example, there were fewer accidents after they introduced the new safety video. For anyone in the public sector, it is a fundamental requirement to be able to prove they somehow achieved good value for money. Second, they should simply like working with you because you are easy to get along with and inspire confidence. Great! But when your contact moves on to new pastures their replacement likely will not know who you are; and they probably won't have any intention of dropping everything to get to know you. So, their only measure of whether they should contact you about their next project is whether your previous work met its objectives. In such circumstances a pleasant "Hello" is not enough, you should gather some solid facts about the effectiveness of the projects you have completed in the past, and remind them what got you onto their *recommended* list.

Now, government-level projects. The quantity of paperwork involved in simply being added to the list of those being considered for the interview process of any kind of governmental undertaking is significant. Okay, I will level with you, it is like nothing you will encounter from any other type of client. I have received 30-page booklets of guidelines to steer me through the complex process of filling in a tender application of equal length. Many of the questions posed within tender applications will seem either baffling or irrelevant, likely because the very same questions are being asked of the suppliers of paperclips. Many of the tenders to which I have drafted responses appeared to have been prepared by people with little or no interest in what they are commissioning. For creatives like us, tenders can feel very cold and dispassionate. During the initial rounds of paperwork your creative solutions are often not sought or are very low on the scoresheet. On many open-tender documents you will see that financial considerations account for 50% or more of the scoring system, with "interpretation of the brief" or "creative ideas and suggestions" accounting for a mere 10%–20% of the scoring criteria. Remember, procurement teams use the tender process to weed out suppliers who would not be able to meet the public sector contract requirements. You will often find your eligibility immediately curtailed by something as mundane as your level of insurance cover, your turnover, trading history, the number of staff you employ, or your sustainability policy.

Always make doubly sure the money on offer is adequate compensation for time and effort you will be putting into delivering the project. Tenders often specify very firm commitments you will be expected to meet; so, read them very carefully indeed. We dropped out of an opportunity to pitch for a lengthy project to produce regular videos for a government website. Hiding within the lengthy tender document was a requirement for weekly reporting meeting with the client. The meeting had to be face-to-face at the department's offices, and this was non-negotiable. We calculated the cost of the roundtrips (hundreds of miles a week) and the enormous time commitment involved to prepare progress reports, and it became clear that the profitability of the commission would take a major hit. Always read the fine details. There will be a lot of stipulations and caveats, some of which may be crucial to deciding whether application is worthwhile.

So—having aired my observations on the process—here is the upside: If the work seems genuinely worthwhile pursuing, then processing the mountain of paperwork can be worth the effort. For several projects we completed for the National Health Service (NHS), the "red tape" involved may have put others off chasing the project. The main benefit of all the investment of your time is that public sector organisations are as secure as any client can get in respect of settling invoices. There is also an element of prestige; it can be reassuring for potential clients to see you have worked with organisations that demand proof of your ability to deliver on your promises.

In summary

- Large public projects are often solely commissioned via online tender platforms. The requirements of major public sector commissions can be arduous. The prerequisites for large tenders might exclude your application from the outset.
- Public sector projects below a set budget threshold can be commissioned at a local level via a "best-value exercise," and there can be far fewer hurdles to clear. There can also be a slight bias—in your favour—for local government departments to commission small businesses in their locality.
- Develop a passion for bureaucratic box-ticking. Public sector projects often require a greater time commitment upfront. It can be a long road to get to the end of the commissioning process. Thankfully, once you have a foot in the door, the ride can be a lot smoother next time round.
- For anyone in the public sector, the ability to prove a project provides good value for money is always a high priority. Do everything you can to help them prove the project you are both working on is worthwhile.
- Throughout your application you should demonstrate not only *what* you intend to deliver, but the exact steps of *how* you will deliver it. Public sector clients require *a lot* of reassurance that you will be able to deliver the work. So, just like you were taught at school "Write down all your

working out"—explicitly state all the milestones in the project and your plan for meeting them.

- When pitching a project to a private business it is possible all the key people will be at the table. In the public sector, you will likely have to accommodate the requirements and input from many other levels of the organisation; people you will likely *never* meet.
- Do not confuse bidding at the lowest price with providing the best value for money. In the public sector, accountability is critical—a proven track record of delivering successful projects on deadline, and within the agreed budget, can be more favourable than merely providing the lowest-cost estimate.
- Getting onto a "recommended supplier" list can be of variable value. Stay in touch with your public sector contacts just as you would any other. When you have proven your worth, make sure you keep reminding people why you are on their list!
- Public sector businesses are mandated to settle invoices on time (in the UK, within 30 days), which is highly advantageous for your cash flow.
- *Hudson Succeed* is a consultancy with a wealth of knowledge in public sector procurement. Hudson's blog provides a generous quantity of helpful guidance for drafting tender applications: www.tenderconsultants.co.uk/writing-winning-bids.

10 Receiving your first brief

So, you have worked around the clock completing the tasks in your comprehensive marketing strategy. You have done an exhausting amount of networking, putting on a few pounds from the canapés you gathered for sustenance during a whirlwind tour of networking functions. But, finally, your hard work has paid off! Someone has sent you a message, they have a possible project they would like your thoughts on. Congratulations!

Now what?

What is a brief?

A brief should be a succinct and carefully considered document explaining the precise objectives of a video commission. A brief should make clear the problems the video must solve, the intended audience, the style it might take, what assets and resources are available, and how the client will measure the success of the production. Often there will be an indication of the budget and deadlines. Other times the client will want to be presented with several creative concepts before deciding exactly how much money they want to allocate to the project; sometimes the production will be taking a portion of a larger budget, so the client will leave division of the budget flexible until they have seen some creative solutions. No matter the scope of the production, no project should begin life without a brief.

Help your client develop their brief

Clients with experience of briefing advertising agencies will usually come to you with objectives that have already been refined and are ready for discussion. I suspect that many of your clients—like mine—will have little or no experience of briefing a video production company. So, it will be down to you to uncover exactly what they are hoping to achieve and assist them in putting together a clear written brief you can all agree on.

Do not be tempted to rush the briefing process. Even when you receive a brief from clients you have worked with several times, there will be unknowns that still need to be explored with them. Most often a potential client will email a loose outline of their objectives, perhaps a link to something they like the look of on YouTube, and other somewhat off-topic questions. This is not yet a fully actionable brief, it is just an introduction. You will have to get back to them to set up a call or a meeting to discuss everything in far more detail. Be wary of potential clients who just want to skip ahead to knowing how much a project is going to cost, or when it can be completed, based *only* on the initial information they have sent you. Every successful project begins by gaining a deep understanding of the client's problems, the solutions that are required, and the measures by which the effectiveness of the project will be gauged. So, you should never provide even "ballpark" prices based on an initial contact that still has a mountain of unexplored variables. Discussing the client's requirements in more detail will usually uncover many additional areas of expense.

The onus is on you to help the client compile a thorough and accurate *written* brief developed from discussion with them. Putting a brief in writing forces everyone to really think about what is required. When a client sees their thoughts written down, they will inevitably see things they want to add or change. The whole aim of this is to get the client to the point where they are saying, "That's it, you're right, you get it." If anything, *you* are going to be helping *them* to clarify their own thoughts on what it is they want to achieve. The time spent developing a refined and precise brief with the client can save time later in the process as it increases the chance your first creative pitch will deliver what the client wants. If the brief is unclear, you will likely waste time devising creative ideas and cost estimates that satisfy the wrong objectives; then you will be back to the drawing board.

If you have seen the BBC series *The Apprentice* featuring Lord Alan Sugar, you'll have seen businesspeople—many boasting of vast expertise in marketing—struggling to create even the most rudimentary TV commercial or promotional video to advertise their fictitious product. Despite the media-rich world we inhabit, most people possess scant understanding of how the creative process operates. Potential clients will, therefore, need a helping hand in getting their ideas together before you can begin working on your creative solutions.

A bespoke project requires a thorough consultation to unearth the answers to questions the client had not yet considered. As the saying goes, "You don't know what you don't know." Therefore, a client's initial brief will always evolve and change direction once you provide your input.

Take the time to understand the problem your client needs to resolve. Yes, every single one of them really does have a "problem" of some kind, even if it is not explicitly made clear at the beginning. Every production you make will be the solution to an issue the client needs to rectify. Sometimes clients may be unable to explain their true need with great clarity, and they will give you an all-encompassing requirement, "We want a video to promote our business," "We want a viral video to put on our Facebook page," "We need a video for our Instagram"—but these are not the true final objective. If you find yourself receiving superficial directions like these, you will need to delve much further into their problem. It is likely there are important unstated facts that have not been raised, possibly because they assume that you—as an experienced producer—must already have figured them out. Dig deeper!

Above all, get your prospective client engaged and excited about briefing you. The quality of their brief determines the quality of what they get from you in return. Some questions you need to ask of any potential client are:

- What problem will this video help you address?
- Who are you trying to reach with this video?
- What outcomes are you hoping to achieve, and how will you measure them?
- What actions do you want your audience to take having viewed the video?
- How are you intending to distribute this video?
- Have you seen something that has inspired you on YouTube?
- Do you envisage the video being produced with motion graphics, or as live action footage?
- Where would you need this to be filmed?
- Do you have an outline script we can progress from, or do you need one written for you?
- Have you had any thoughts about the type of voice that you would like to narrate this?
- Are there any brand guidelines for your business that we should adhere to?
- Are you working within a fixed budget, or is this still undecided?
- When do you need ideas back from us?
- When is your deadline for completing the project?

You may notice one question by its absence, "How long should the video be?" I have asked this many times, and it has prompted peculiar—often unhelpful—responses. People each have their own unique grasp of time, especially when it comes to imagining the duration of something that does not yet exist. The duration they would specify often seemed to be just plucked out of the air, and sometimes they would get quite attached to the duration they had expressed. Most times they would shoot high—usually north of ten minutes—even for a message that could easily be conveyed in just a couple of minutes or less. For me, the question of duration has proven not to be a particularly useful steer. The length of a production is an area where it is best to set the client's expectations from your own professional experience, rather than putting the topic up for debate. Explain your reasoning for approximate durations when you pitch your creative solutions.

There are only two scenarios where I would delve into specific requirements relating to duration:

First: Paid advertising placements. Productions for advertising purposes will usually have to meet a very exact specification, and on social media there will usually be a *maximum* duration. Often, clients will not know the specifications, but if you get the names of all the platforms they want to be on, the recommended and maximum durations are just a Google away.

Second: Videos for use at events which must run to a predetermined schedule, such as a conference. We produced a video for a client's meeting with a potential venture fund investor, the video presentation had to be exactly five minutes or less, not one single second longer would be acceptable. The script was hacked-back to only the most pertinent messages and was comfortably delivered at four and a half minutes.

If anything, the better question to ask might be "Is there a maximum duration the video must not exceed?" In all other cases just stick to the golden rule: Do not let anything run for a second longer than it remains good to watch!

If the potential client has a greater understanding of briefing creative businesses, they might introduce themselves to you by sending you an almost fully formed brief. This demonstrates they have already put some thought into their objectives, and the project is more than just speculative. A comprehensive brief has often been created to allow the client to skip the need for repeated initial discussions with production companies. This is sometimes referred to as a "Request to Pitch" or an "Invitation to Quote," and it will often get sent out to multiple producers. In my experience it is common practice for a potential client to have sent the same brief to three to four production companies.

Good briefs will have had plenty of thought put into them, but keep in mind that briefs are often written by people still in the process of formulating their own ideas; and they have presumably approached you on the basis of the additional creative input you can bring to the party. As such, you will often find small omissions, contradictions, or incorrect terminologies.

So, what might an initial brief from a legitimate potential client look like? Well, it just so happens I have a *real* email right here:

From: potential.client@acme.inc
To: best.producer@brilliantproductionco.com
Subject: Fitness Products Showcase Videos

Hello, I hope you are having a good week?

We are looking at how we reach out to existing and new buyers to showcase our company, ACME Inc, and our range of products. Recipients of the videos are in the fitness industry, and it is the retail buyers in this sector who will be our target audience. It all needs to be professional but have a strong fun/wow factor to it. We are speaking with video production agencies about delivering the following:

- 5–10 minute sales presentation video to host on our website and to send out to buyers, so it acts as an introductory sales presentation for next year's product range.
- We would like to also be able to have approx. 5–10 shorter video clips that we can email out.
- We would like included in the video footage, a "walk around" of our different product categories: dietary supplements, bulk powders, professional equipment, and domestic (home) fitness equipment, and others—all can be identified and expanded upon in a fuller brief if the project is agreed.
- We would like to include footage that highlights the products in our showroom, with close-ups of specific products, voice over, and text added to the footage.
- We would like small interview/demonstration style segments with our Marketing Director to be included.
- Music added for background would be required.
- Some graphics and effects would be nice to incorporate into the footage to add extra excitement to the product ranges.
- We think 1-day of filming at our offices in Big City will be enough.
- How many days editing do you think would be required?
- If you can provide demonstration staff, in case our Marketing Director would prefer not to be filmed, can you let us know a cost on using a professional person?

At this stage we are looking to receive estimates on the production, and the timings involved. We hope to then present these to our Directors and, if greenlit, we'd be looking to begin the project quite quickly in the next 2–3 weeks. If you need any further information or want to run through the above, I'm happy to set up a call.

Best regards,
Potential Client

Awesome! This is a great start! Sure, there are gaps in the requirements and a few unclear requests, otherwise plenty of thought has gone into it. The aims of the project are reasonably well defined and are described at length *before* mention of cost. The disclosure that other producers have also received the brief makes it even more credible. Most positive of all, the project has a sense of urgency and the prospect is open to discussing their requirements in more detail. This is a brief with genuine potential for turning into a paid project. Arrange that call right away!

Now... let us compare that delightful brief to another I received (typos uncorrected)—

> **From**: kris.iffy@sketchybiz.nope
> **To:** best.producer@brilliantproductionco.com
> **Subject**: video cost
>
> I work for Sketchy Biz, we make an anti-aging product. I have been asked by my boss to look into the potential of creating a marketing video, at the moment there are a lot of things undecided, so this is in the preliminary stages. The objectives are to reach the people that don't know much about our kind of product. We currently look into costings of creating and placing the video, and there will need to be further discussions internally about what direction we need to go in and whether it its feasible. We have seen a advert created my one of our competitors—*https://youtu.be/wildly-expensive-tv-campaign* Because this is something we haven't really thought about before or done would it be possible to get an estimate of how much something similar would cost to make. In addition if you do know what sort of costs would be involved with gettibg people to see this, potentially because of our business, we are thinking makeup tutorials on YouTube or maybe show it on TV during programmes for older people?
>
> Thanks.
> Kris

Red. Flags. Everywhere. Can you figure out what Kris needs? I can't. I don't think even Kris knows what he's trying to achieve. And even if he did, I strongly doubt he'd have the money to achieve it. I looked at the video Kris sent and gave him an idea how much it likely cost. Kris never replied.

Disassembling a (good) brief

My personal method is to go through the brief with a highlighter, plucking out the most pertinent points which need to be addressed in our response to the potential client. Yes, print it out on paper! When viewing documents on-screen it can be too easy to scroll through at speed, skim-reading, and missing something important. As I'm highlighting, I will be making a bullet point "criteria we must meet" list. I can then tick items off this list as I draft the pitch to make sure that every query has been thoroughly answered or has been queried with the potential client. Never assume that anything in a brief is there just for the sake of it. If a question is raised in the brief—even if it might appear to be a minor throwaway point—always address it. It reassures the recipient that you have thoroughly read and considered *everything* they sent to you.

Also, pay very close attention to the tiniest of details your prospective client is expecting in return. A brief we responded to just a few days ago had a small caveat in the last paragraph:

> Your proposal should be returned electronically no later than midday on Tuesday 4th July, no more than 4 pages please.

The project in question was a large undertaking, the pitch would have to cover a lot of detail, and I wondered how many of the production companies responding to the brief would inadvertently send pitches far more than the specified four pages. I am sure some potential clients place small requests within their briefs as a slightly sadistic—or rather cunning—method of weeding out those who lack an eye for detail. I totally get it. I once removed a potential supplier from my shortlist when they sent a proposal where all the elements they had copied and pasted from another proposal appeared in a different typeface.

I digress. As the adage goes, "The way you do something is the way you do anything." Go through briefs with attention to the very smallest of details. List the information the client is requesting, look for any deliberate "traps," and continually refer back to the brief while working on your pitch. Keep asking, "Is my pitch *truly* answering the brief?" Above all, always get other people's eyes on the pitch for their observations, typos, grammar checks, and unfiltered critique before the final document gets sent. Several times I have gone back to the drawing board on a pitch because a couple of people viewing the document through fresh eyes said, "Sorry, but I just didn't quite get it."

When "how much?" is the client's first question

One of the first questions many potential clients will ask at the briefing stage is "How much will it cost?" While sometimes a red flag, oftentimes this question comes from a genuine place. If the prospective client has never commissioned a creative project, cost may seem an obvious place for them to open the discussion. You need move them toward discussing their requirements and refining the brief. They will begin to appreciate that the many variables involved make it impossible to give an upfront price. When their brief starts to take shape, they will be comfortable providing an indication of the budget they can commit to the project.

We have a fun little rouse for discovering how much money is really on the table. Let's say the briefing feels genuine, the client is enthusiastic, but they tell you, "We've not really thought much about the budget at this stage." Your response—delivered with tremendous enthusiasm—could be "Brilliant, we love it when there's scope on the budget, we can really do something daring!" They will want to temper your enthusiasm, "Oh, well we really wouldn't want to spend any more than..."

Beware potential clients for whom price is the overriding or only topic of discussion. An unwavering pushiness to be given a price, or even "just a ball-park cost" before committing the time to discuss their objectives in greater depth can sometimes be the sign of a project that has already been discussed with other parties, or is at a highly speculative stage. If you are confident that you have got enough information to go on, and the potential client is still pushing for an idea of price before they'll discuss a project further you can tell them "You're looking at a budget broadly in the area of..." and give them a single round amount, shooting high, and ask if that tallies with their expectations. Try not to provide a client with an upper and lower range of prices, because they will only ever remember the lower of the two amounts and get fixated on working down to that figure. If the project is genuine, discussion will continue. If they want to wrap up discussion soon after hearing a price, you will likely never hear from them again.

Very occasionally we have had to decline providing estimates to businesses that either have a long-standing incumbent producer or have made multiple last-minute "We just need quick a price for a meeting we're heading to" calls. Once provided with an estimate they become evasive and hard to contact. Months later, unsurprisingly, we will see their regular supplier has done the work, probably having been beaten down on price by our estimate.

Double-check the budget

At this stage you should have been successful in reassuring your prospective client that you get what they are all about, and you fully understand their objectives. You have got the pitching process off to a flying start.

Hopefully, you have ascertained the client's range of movement on budget or have even got a firm figure from which to develop your creative approach. Before the conversation is done—even if you *think* you noted the budget correctly—always circle back and make sure to check the budget once again. Why should you double-check? Well, we were called on to put together a high-level proposal for refreshing the video marketing strategy of a collective of European universities. To deliver the numerous required productions—filmed across several countries—would have been a complex undertaking. We spent more than a week putting together a very thorough response to their brief. We were confident of being, at the very least, shortlisted for a follow-up call. We felt the time we had invested in the pitch had been well-spent considering the generous £100,000 budget for the project.

We sent our beautifully crafted, critiqued, and proofread PDF into the ether and waited for a couple of months, patiently respecting the potential client's "Don't call us, we'll call you" order. By the way, when a client specifies "We'll call you," be patient with them. They know better than yourself how long their internal processes will take to grind through all the proposals. Academic and government organisations often work by committees that only congregate at set intervals, so cut them some slack. Eventually we got a response from the committee, and it was just a couple of curt sentences. They had flat-out declined to look at our proposal, tossing it aside as it was far beyond their stated budget.

What!? Seriously? Had we majorly dropped the ball somewhere on this one? We went back to review the briefing document. The brief exhaustively covered every detail—*except* for the budget. So, where had the rogue £100k figure come from? Trawling back through our exchange of emails, the budget had been stated by the client's UK agency only once, in their first email to us. The budget seemed generous, but nonetheless accurate considering the complexity of the work that was going to be involved. So, £100k was accepted as fact and everything from that point onwards was developed within that budget. Unfortunately, there had been some confusion at the client's agency when converting the budget from Euros to Sterling, which had then been further compounded by some ambiguous wording and a typo. Our carefully constructed proposal—that had seemingly hit the budget on the nail—was £20,000 *over budget*. The agency apologised for the confusion, but the client had already awarded the project to another production company that had worked from correct information.

Lesson learned: Always *double-check* the budget, especially if it seems oddly generous.

When your potential client reveals they have a roster of producers

When a request to pitch for a project arrives in your inbox it can pay dividends to spend a few minutes Googling the prospective client. Try to find existing videos that have been produced for them. These can provide a handy steer as to the client's resources and possible expectations. Assuming their existing videos are of a good quality, you might wonder why they are contacting you. They might have experienced bad chemistry with the producer and ended the relationship. Or, just maybe, they want to add you to a roster of producers.

It is not uncommon for very large businesses to form relationships with several producers, or to retain multiple advertising agencies, splitting large workloads into individual areas of expertise. At one of our larger clients, several specialist agencies get a slice of the marketing department's budget. One agency handles marketing collateral, another specialises in public-facing advertising, a third exclusively produces work for incentive schemes and annual conferences, and a fourth handles PR and social media. A well-served healthy client is good news for all its suppliers.

Nine times out of ten your research into a prospective client will reveal that producers you are familiar with have worked with them in the past, or still appear to be a current provider. Working on the same patch as other producers may feel uncomfortable to begin with, but it is quite a common scenario when dealing with large businesses who can offer plenty of opportunities to go round. When a business feels they have assembled a team of experts that play well *together* to provide the best results, you will find yourself in an enviable position.

So, the client wants to brief you face-to-face

A face-to-face discussion is a positive indicator that a prospective client might be serious about a project and is willing to invest some time in taking things forward. It also demonstrates that the client wants to get a feel for the type of working relationship they could form with you.

We prepare for a client meeting by having sometimes two, even three, internal meetings beforehand. We read through whatever brief the prospect has already sent over, pull together what we know about the new contact and their business, do background research, and put together a list of questions to put to the potential client for clarification. The goal of a briefing meeting is just the same as for a brief by any other means, it serves to get yourself and the client on the same page about the project's objectives. And, it should also result in the creation of a document that everyone can reference.

What if "face-to-face" is "hop on a Zoom call?"

For many years video conferencing was the preserve of boardrooms in multinational businesses. If you did not have access to such luxury you were relegated to dialling into a conference call. Conference call systems were—and often still are—terrible quality and not at all conducive to smooth multi-person discussions. Then Zoom arrived, and the blame for unflattering lighting and awful audio quality shifted directly onto the individuals in the call. Zoom and the like are the natural successor to clunky conference calls. Businesses are now less inclined to travel without good cause, and they are also more open to using suppliers they might never meet in person (which is great for the future of remote work).

So, I believe it is now a competitive advantage to not only be flexible in the channels you use to communicate, but to be able to use them with a technical proficiency that demonstrates your grasp of the very medium you are discussing with your potential client! If you are discussing a high-gloss video production, do not appear on a Zoom call as a dark silhouette, in an echoing room, with the camera pointing up your nostrils. Rig yourself some flattering lighting, install some acoustic sound dampening, buy a pro audio interface and a condenser microphone to override your device's built-in audio. Yes, improving your setup might not be cheap, but achieving pristine audio and video quality for all your calls is—in my opinion—part of your brand positioning. You will also be less reluctant to join video calls because your contributions to the conversation will look awesome! You are selling video production services; it follows that your Zoom (or Microsoft Teams) calls should have superb video and audio quality. For my Zoom calls I use a Focusrite Scarlett interface with a studio condenser microphone, and a DSLR attached to my PC with an Elgato Camlink interface. Root out and squish all technical issues that could stall your calls. If you are getting freezing, dropped frames, or audio glitches, do not just assume the app is at fault—try to trace the problem and make sure it is not your setup that is at fault. I solved 99% of my issues with video calls by ditching my Wi-Fi and using a hardwired Ethernet connection.

When a brief is not really a brief at all

When you have been in the production business awhile you will sometimes find yourself approached by a major brand or advertising agency that you secretly suspect is a little out of your league. They will have found you seemingly at random, not via a referral or any previous contact, and they'll remain cagey about their budget or the identity of their end client. They will tell you it is a massive opportunity, and they need "your absolute best price" for the project. There is another caveat, they do not need any creative from you right now, but they do urgently require a ballpark estimate. This might be a type of "longlisting." Essentially someone is just putting the feelers out for producers to pad out a list of estimates for a highly speculative project—i.e. they are delegating the footwork to respond to a brief they do not believe has much chance of going ahead.

I do not wish to dampen your enthusiasm, because just sometimes amazing opportunities *really do* randomly drop from the sky. A far more credible scenario would be that one of your prior happy clients has referred you to the "out of your league" client, or have themselves gone to work for them, in which case you should be falling over yourself to grasp the opportunity.

Run a background check

You should always be seeking premium clients; those who value your work and have the willingness and ability to pay for it. We are fortunate to have accumulated a superb lineup of very professional repeat clients; you should also be able to feel good about the clients you are serving. The best professionals prefer to work with only the best clients. Very occasionally you will be approached by a client who gives you a gut-feeling there is something not quite right. Maybe their product or service sounds a bit dubious, or their market research is trying to prove claims that sound too good to be true. If something feels amiss about a potential client, or you just get bad vibes from something they have said, run a background check. I am sure that sounds harsh or underhanded, but it really is a sensible precaution.

A background check on a potential client can be as simple as searching Google, LinkedIn, and social networks to check out their reputation. If you are still not satisfied, you can look at their reporting history and corporate structure (in the UK) on the Companies House website. Have they been established for several years with the same directors at the helm? Or has the company name changed several times with flakey directors coming and going, or are there fines for late filing of documents? We once gave the benefit of doubt to a client whose product had made us feel somewhat uncomfortable, but they appeared otherwise legitimate. Weeks later they went bust owing an outstanding invoice; after that incident we stepped up our checks and began using the paid financial analysis service DueDil.com. This platform provides deep insights into the management and financial state of more than 50 million companies.

If something concerns you about a potential client, you will not be acting unprofessionally in any way whatsoever in doing research. It is entirely prudent to err on the side of caution.

In summary

- Every great project begins with a thorough brief. A quick discussion with a potential client is *not* a brief. You need to create a *written* outline detailing the scope of the project and its requirements before you begin forming creative solutions.
- Keep asking questions until the client's problems and their objectives are entirely clear. A good brief must get the client and yourself on the same page about what the project needs to achieve. This is important because of the huge degree of subjectivity in creative projects.
- Resist the temptation to provide even "ballpark" prices at the outset. Clients will remember the first figure you gave them, especially when you later take a more thorough brief and cost the project at twice the amount you initially stated!
- It *is* natural for clients to ask about price early in the process. But if getting an estimate from you becomes an overriding topic of discussion (while they stubbornly avoid revealing their budget range) you need to discover why the need for an upfront price is such a high priority so early in discussion.
- A lack of questions from the potential client, and a reluctance to spend time going into details can be a sign you are a non-contender, a late consideration, or that the project is highly speculative. Over time you will be able to tune your gut-feeling to pick up on what is going on.
- Make the briefing process enjoyable, get the client fully engaged and talking about their business and their project. The chances of the client receiving a pitch—and later a production—that they are delighted with are greatly increased by their willingness to put significant thought into their requirements.
- Get them to show you some examples of something they like on YouTube. This seems to be the norm for many clients without need to prompt them. It can be a useful illustration of their ambitions for the project. Set

aside the high likelihood these examples will show work far beyond their means, and ask them about the specific production details that appeal to them—"Do you like the music?" "Do you like the editing style?" "Do you like the way the text fills the screen?" Find a way to translate the elements they are enthusiastic about into requirements in the brief.

- Assist the client in developing their brief further, explore details they have not investigated. They don't know what they don't know. It is very rare that even the most detailed brief from a client does not raise further questions you will need answers to.
- Keep asking questions until you have a thorough understanding of the client's requirements. Do not be concerned about asking "obvious" questions, the answers to them might be more important than you anticipate.
- At the briefing stage, clients often confuse their objectives for the project with their overall business objectives. If you are provided with general goals like "We want more traffic to our site" or "We want more enquiries" you will need to narrow the focus of the brief.
- Filling the blanks in a brief is the first opportunity to delve deep into the potential client's business. Take an interest, show that you are really intrigued by their requirements. Begin building a relationship that demonstrates you care about their success.
- All briefs are an expression of a problem that needs to be solved. If you can fully understand the problem, you will be better able to provide a creative pitch that demonstrates the perfect solution to the problem.
- Investing time in getting the brief correct increases the chances of your creative pitch meeting the client's needs at the first attempt. Establishing clear criteria also reduces the risks of wasted effort developing creative solutions that met the wrong objectives.
- Unless a production must clearly be restricted to a specific duration, do not get hung up on finding out from the client how long a production should run. The duration should be decided by your creative solution, and not an arbitrary number suggested by the client.
- Some clients will have taken the time to write a clearly explained and comprehensive brief of their requirements. Read it properly. Consider it carefully. If it helps, do this on paper with a highlighter. When a client has taken the time to craft a substantial and exhaustive briefing document, it is highly unlikely that you are the *only* recipient!
- Create a checklist of exactly what information the brief is asking of you and use it to check that your pitch addresses all the points on the list. This is another example of why it is so important to *always* have a *written* brief for continual reference.
- Pay close attention to the smallest of details in a brief. Very occasionally, a brief assembled by a particularly bureaucratic variety of client might even specify the length and formatting your response should take. They will appreciate that you have taken the time to make their job easier by playing the game.

- Double-check the budget before starting work on your creative ideas, sometimes the budget will have mysteriously changed by the second time you ask!
- Communicate with the client in whatever method they find easiest, even if they refuse to budge from a dial-in conference call! Where you can, opt for a video call. Make a reassuring impression by establishing a killer camera and mic setup that you can rely on to perform flawlessly. Make sure you are familiar with the operation of all the current apps.
- The best professionals prefer to work with only the best clients. If something about the prospect's business or service gives you bad vibes, it is entirely professional to do some digging into the legitimacy of their business.

11 Production budgets

Decide your pricing strategy

You must establish benchmark rates for all the less variable elements of your offering; what you charge for an hour of your time, or a whole day. How much you charge for a day of editing, or for a day of motion-graphics production. These rates should be kept consistent across every project. Adjusting rate-card prices between clients can cause nightmarish financial analysis and forecasting (more on this later!).

It is going to be tough to establish a pricing strategy that feels a fair reward for the value your work provides, while also covering your overheads and generating profit. Most likely, you will assume the rates you are coming up with are above average. Well, I suspect your rates are not that high at all, and you are likely being rather conservative. Remember, your domestic finances are worlds apart from those of a business. Wouldn't it be irritating to discover the reason your clients keep working with you is because you are ridiculously underpricing yourself? There is an old maxim among salespeople: If the client doesn't hesitate to say "Yes" when the price is presented to them, you didn't ask for enough! Your pricing structure forms a part of your reputation. Professionals in high demand are—to quote the slogan of a popular brand of beer—"reassuringly expensive." You're a professional of genuine integrity. You do not churn out rubbish that is not going to be effective for the client.

Abir Syed of Upcounting points out three important angles from which to view your price strategy,

> The first [consideration] is obviously the market. Most people who are searching for a service will get a quote from more than one place, so it is important to know what pricing is out there from competitors who offer a comparable quality and have comparable experience. You don't need to compare against all options out there, so focus on your marketplace. If you go speak to local businesses, they'll likely find your competitors on the first page of Google. If you are sending proposals on a freelancer marketplace like Upwork, then those are the competitors your prospective clients will consider. Second, is your 'opportunity cost'. You should

> consider what else you could be doing, whether that be administrative work for your video production company, or lower value client work that would be more worthy of your time than taking a given opportunity. Those other opportunities make up the lowest pricing you should be willing to accept for a given project. That is also impacted though by your capacity.

In short, if the time you spend on marketing your business would generate more income than the client project you're currently working on, the minimum amount you charge for client work should be far greater than the value of the time you spend elsewhere.

Abir adds,

> Your capacity will determine whether you should stick to a higher pricing scheme and be willing to walk away from a project, or if you should take on the work anyway, because you have a lot of free capacity. That is usually true as long as you also pay attention to your cost.

As an example, we received an enquiry from a fashion retailer with a brief to produce a video featuring their outfits. We put together a quick estimate to produce something that would meet their brief, it came to around £7,000. They sent an email back to us asking what we would be able to do with a maximum budget of £1,000. We were between productions at that moment, and we could have done *something* for that amount of money. But—in all honesty—we would not have been especially happy with the result, and the client would not have had their true vision realised. Yes, we would have a grand in the bank; and yes, we probably would have scraped a small profit, but ultimately the project was one that we could not take on. Our time could be spent on more valuable tasks.

I asked Marilyn Heywood Paige, CMO of Paige Black, about pricing strategies in the marketing sector. Marilyn suggested that one of the shortcuts to understanding your market positioning could be to gain the experience from within a business you might later wish to emulate,

> The quickest way to be successful with your own production company is to go work for a production company that already has the kind of corporate clients you hope will hire your firm someday. Let someone else pay you to make mistakes and learn the ropes of working with them. Pay attention to the relationships between the creative team and the client. Ask questions about what the corporate client needs to accomplish, and why the creative team chooses the solutions that they do. Get familiar with budgets and timelines. Learn everything you can about providing video services to the corporate clients on someone else's dime before diving into the responsibilities of your own production house.

Keep your enthusiasm in check

When costing projects, it can be easy to get led off course by your enthusiasm for the brief, the desire to win the pitch, and to see your great idea through to completion. At times you will devise an ingenious creative concept that would push the bounds of your client's upper budget. But, goddam, it *would* be exciting to shoot, and it *would* look great on the showreel! You will then try to find ways to make the cost more palatable for the client by cutting your margins; this is where you run the risk of your client choosing the concept that would make your business the *least* profit. We are all guilty of wanting to lower an estimate to mitigate the pain of losing a project we would have really enjoyed working on. However, putting in place a structured method of costing all your projects—and sticking to it—can safeguard against any emotional bias as it will show you, in clear numbers, how the project stacks up financially.

How to cost creative solutions objectively

Make Excel, Numbers, or Google Sheets your new best friend. Create a template spreadsheet that you will *always* use to cost every one of your creative concepts, for every one of your potential clients. *Never* skip the spreadsheet! Standardisation maintains accuracy and objectiveness, and it will also save you a lot of time.

Your spreadsheet template must be formatted to demonstrate the profitability of every stage of production. Running down the first column of your spreadsheet, list every element of the production journey in chronological order. The beginning of the project will be on the top line, with final delivery and sundry costs at the bottom of the column. To the right of each line item you will need to fill the time requirements for this project (hours and days), the sum cost to you, and the higher cost that you will charge to the client. The difference between the two costs is your mark-up, and this should be expressed as a percentage. You should be able to vary the percentage of mark-up for each line item independently and have the cost-to-client column calculate accordingly. Working with percentages—in addition to cash amounts—in your sheet prompts you to consider your mark-ups more objectively.

Remember, *every* task that needs to be performed to bring a creative concept to reality *must* have a line on the spreadsheet, because it undoubtedly has a financial cost associated with it. Even if you plan on spending a couple of hours in a coffee shop planning the logistic of a shoot, you will still be paying yourself a salary during that time, and your hourly cost to the business needs to be represented on the sheet; the same goes for the activities of anyone else you have on your team.

You must *always* mark-up each cost *individually* (especially your internal overheads) to make them each show a profit. It is a rookie error to put all the elements onto the sheet at-cost and simply add a fixed profit mark-up to the total amount. Do not take this shortcut, you will lose critical insight into your cost structure. The profit margin percentage at the bottom line should be automatically calculating from the mark-ups on each line in the sheet as you fill them. This way, if your Director of Photography later specifies an additional lens or light to their initial requirements, you can punch in the extra cost on the sheet and it will automatically calculate the resulting hit to the profit margin.

We get very granular on our costing sheet; you should add as much detail as required to capture all the costs that will be associated with delivering the production. You need a true understanding of the likely profitability of the concept you intend to pitch to the client. Let us say you find it impossible to draft a good script without first ordering a couple of pizzas and a six-pack. Hey, I'm not judging. If this is the process you use to get the job done—and you anticipate ordering two large Hawaiians with extra pineapple for the project you are currently pricing—then the hourly rate you set for your scriptwriting must already incorporate these "catering expenses." The reason for such precision will become clear in the next section.

Our costing sheet follows a template like this (each bullet represents a cell in the leftmost column):

Pre-production (internal)

- Project management (client liaison, booking equipment and crew, admin)
- Internal team meetings and brainstorm sessions
- Scriptwriting
- Development and design of client pitch

Production (internal)

- Producer/Director
- Production Assistant
- Account Handler (client liaison)

Production (freelance)

- Director of Photography
- Camera Operator
- Camera Assistant
- Sound Recordist
- Makeup/Stylist

Production equipment (internal)

- Standard basic lighting kit
- C-stands and sandbags
- Standard grip (tripod, fluid head, high-hat)

Production equipment (external rental)

- Camera kit (camera body, lenses, batteries, location monitor)
- Specialist lighting kit

- Specialist grip
- Equipment delivery and insurance

Post-production vision (internal)

- OCF (Original Camera File) ingest, backup, metadata tagging
- Video Editor
- Director (post-production rate)

Post-production sound (internal)

- Music and voice artist research
- Sound Engineer

Licensing (external)

- Stock photography purchases
- Stock video purchases
- Music licensing
- Voiceover fees
- In-vision performers (actors) fees

Sundries (external)

- Additional insurance
- Props hire or purchase
- Location catering/lunches
- Hotels/overnights
- LTO (Linear Tape-Open) backup tapes and offsite archival

Mileage (external)

- Crew vehicle
- Freelance vehicle 1
- Freelance vehicle 2

Profit margin

You should *not* simply be calculating the profitability of the individual production; you must be factoring (by design of your costing sheet) how the profitability of the project would contribute to your wider business picture. Essentially, you have *two* profit margins to consider: The profit margin within the individual project and the profit margin of your wider business.

Once you have filled the expenditure and mark-up for these items the bottom-line calculations of your estimate should show the total fees due for your *internal costs* (line items relating to your own time or equipment) and the total fees for *external costs* (the time of others, rented equipment, travel, etc.) each inclusive of their mark-ups.

Lastly, to the total of these fees you should also add a percentage of contingency for additional costs that will arise during production, because they always will. Ten percent is usually ample.

Your estimate might well demonstrate that some of the creative concepts you fell in love with would go far beyond the client's budget, or they would squeeze your profit margin to such a degree that it would not make commercial sense to present them to your client. Presenting creative ideas that are *slightly* above the client's budget is a judgement call; this is where gaining a good brief and an understanding of the client's resources will help you decide whether to put forward an over-budget concept. Are they likely to be open-minded? We usually present three creative solutions in a pitch. The first two will always be within the scope of the client's brief. The third solution we present can—if needed—be a wildcard, more edgy and daring but still meeting the client's objectives. The wildcard idea can be a little over budget with justifiable reasons. Note, I said a *little* over budget. Try not to present something so outrageously far from the brief that it appears self-serving. You must be confident that if the client commissions you to produce any of the concepts, then all of them will meet or exceed the set percentage of profit margin you need for your business.

Having confidence in your estimate

If your client has set an immovable budget, and the cash is already signed-off as theirs to spend, your estimating job will be made easier. If the estimates for your creative solutions are on-budget—and you can do the work above your minimum acceptable profit margin—you are good to go!

Calculating a cost estimate for a pitch to a client whose brief had a wider scope and a more flexible budget often raises an unexpected emotional stumbling block. You might find it a struggle to justify the final price of the estimate to yourself, and inadvertently pre-empt your client requesting cuts to the budget. The cost is the cost, the profit margin is fair, but for some reason you feel a slight pang of guilt when looking at the total figure. You wonder, "Am I asking for too much?" You will consider dropping your estimate in the hope of winning an enjoyable project. You tell yourself, "This will be really nice for our reel." The root of this feeling is that you enjoy your work so much that you feel guilty asking for money in return for your talent. Such is the temptation to undervalue your creative services—or even to work at a loss—to get a gig that would be enjoyable to work on. Some producers appear to earn a living while spending every day doing pro bono projects for the sheer pleasure of it. Abir Syed is a Digital Marketing Consultant in Montreal,

> Probably the biggest [mindset shift] is to not think of your own time as free. A freelancer might only think of costs in terms of what *they* must pay. But once you have a team, any time you spend on one activity can mean having to pay someone to take care of *another* activity. Attributing a value to your own time and making decisions as though you have to pay yourself as an employee can help with achieving that mindset.

Don't give away too much for the budget

Jason Cherubini is Chief Operating and Financial Officer of Dawn's Light Media. He is also an accounting academic and serial entrepreneur. In another reminder that the world of entertainment has many crossovers with that of commercial video production, Jason points out a truth that creatives working across all varieties of media often find difficult to take on board,

> Being passionate about projects is for amateurs, not for professionals. As a professional, every choice needs to be evaluated on a cost-benefit basis. What will this particular choice cost, and how much will it benefit us? So, there may be some choices that would be artistically beautiful, but very expensive. Unless that increase in artistic beauty increases the revenue, it shouldn't be done. This doesn't mean that all artistry should be avoided, but it needs to be evaluated from a financial perspective.

An estimate should always cover your operating overheads and the costs incurred during the production, with built-in margins of error as contingency and—of course—a healthy profit. No business can look forward to a bright future without consistently operating profitably.

One way to figure out whether you are undershooting or overshooting with your estimate is to consider your client's resources, and the tangible value of the project as it relates to their objectives, or bottom line. What value will your finished production provide them? Abir Syed added,

> You should try to frame your offering in terms of how much value you can bring to the customer, rather than how much it will cost them. A client that will use a video you produce as a Facebook ad that can generate large amounts of revenue can achieve a higher return on investment from the video than a client who just wants to use it as a one-time social media post.

We were involved in a production for a local government department. The final product was a video training package to help children develop the confidence to use public transport to get to school. The desired outcome would reduce reliance on state-funded school transport and cut road congestion around schools. The department estimated the potential financial savings to be in the order of several hundred-thousand pounds. With those potential savings in mind it was possible to form an idea of the size of budget the department would consider a good investment. The project was estimated, with a healthy profit margin, to cost £30,000—a sizeable job for us, and a modest and justifiable investment for the department, who would possess an effective and valuable training package for several years to come.

Balancing the value that a production may hold for your potential client, versus its actual production costs, can also indicate whether the project may be a non-starter.

I was approached by a burgeoning record label embarking on its first live music festival. The label wanted to shoot the festival as a promotional tool for the second event they hoped to run. I met with the promoters to discuss the size of the undertaking. I always take plenty of notes, even of details that at first do not appear relevant to the brief. From the promoters I gathered that advance tickets were £15, with walk-up tickets available on the day for £10. The venue allowed a maximum attendance of 525. I also knew that the performers on the billing had needed some encouragement to commit to an unknown label running an untested event; they had insisted on payment upfront, and rooms at good hotels. A quick calculation showed that even in the very best scenario the event would take less than £8,000 in ticket sales, and much of that had likely already been speculatively spent to secure the artists and venue. Also, as a first outing without a loyal following it was unlikely to be a sell-out. Factoring other costs such as insurance, equipment, lighting rig, security, and so forth, I figured the event might just make a small profit. The promoters no doubt saw my work as being of promotional value to them, but it was not likely to carry any significant monetary value. Neither the promoter nor I was going to see any tangible financial benefit from the production. The value for them simply did not stack up against the actual billable costs that would have been involved. Disclaimer: I did the project in my own time and was paid with a bottle of Jack Daniels. It did not make financial sense, but it was a memorable shoot.

Working pro bono for "exposure"

Doing a freebie can make *strategic* sense in *certain* scenarios. For example, if you find yourself frequently fielding enquiries for a style of work that you are confident you would be able to deliver but lack any examples that are of an appropriate style. After losing a few gigs to producers who had more relevant work on their reels, you can consider the cost of doing a project for free as a marketing expense. We did a freebie a couple of years ago when several potential client briefs would have suited a stop-motion animation treatment, but it had been 25 years since we had last created anything remotely similar. We approached a local business whose products suited a stop-motion animation and created a piece for our reel at no cost to them. The short animation has been a valuable marketing asset and has paid for itself several times over. When you *choose* to do a "showreel piece" on favourable—or even free—terms for a client, always make sure at the outset that they will be happy for you to use the finished video in your marketing, and that they will be willing to provide a testimonial. Jason Cherubini of Dawn's Light Media is also very sceptical of the value of merely giving your skills away for exposure,

> The idea of working for exposure is a horrible idea. It shows that you don't value your work. Do a little research into what comparable people are charging for the work you do and develop your pricing off of that. This doesn't mean that you will never offer discounts or do favors on

> projects that will help your career, but those should be the exception and not the rule. If someone isn't willing to value your work and pay you for it now, they never will. And the only people they will 'expose' you to are other people who will want you to work for free.

Jason's last observation is especially true. Just sometimes the beneficiary of your generosity *will* return the favour and be a cheerleader for your services. But promoting *you* is *not* their job, and they will soon forget the effort you put in at your own expense. If you choose to work for exposure, *you* are the one who must generate that exposure and make the video work hard as an item of marketing collateral.

Beware of discounting

Giving away your time at-cost, or at a financial loss, can also bring with it the additional problem of warping your view of what the market needs. People will gladly use your services when you are giving them away for free—from their perspective they've nothing to lose—and it is easy to convince yourself that their interest equates to an enthusiastic and untapped marketplace. Often, their initial enthusiasm will dry-up when you need to begin charging them. Giving away freebies can convince you of the existence of a market that really does not exist.

Also, promoting unfeasibly low rates or immediately cutting your estimate at the first sign of pushback from a client shifts your positioning toward the bottom end of the market. At a networking event a young guy introduced himself to me and offered to design a website for just £45. When someone offers a service at a price which causes me to wonder how they can afford to feed or clothe themselves I do not put much faith in the service they would be providing. He might as well have said, "My work isn't at all good, so I'm going to justify a mediocre effort by giving it to you for nothing." Seen from that perspective, why would I get excited about someone offering to work for beer money? Jason Cherubini agrees that pricing your expertise far below industry average can serve to make you unattractive to the very clients you are trying to attract,

> A few years ago, I was contacted by an alumnus of my alma mater. He had completed law school, and worked in law for a couple of years, but he wanted to set out on his own targeting the entertainment industry. He wasn't having much luck in securing clients. After meeting with him, it came out that he was offering his services at a third of the price of his competition. He thought by offering a low price, he would have seen a lot of people coming to him to take advantage of the cost savings, but it wasn't happening. I explained to him that most people will judge the value of what they are getting based on the price they pay for it. His price being so low gave his potential customers the impression that he wasn't a good lawyer and wasn't worth even the reduced fee. After he raised his

fee back to the industry standard, he saw an increase in demand. To seal new clients, he chose to selectively offer discounts on his industry standard pricing, but he made sure it was clear that it was a one-time discount.

Never lose sight of your position—or aspiration—in the marketplace. When I require a problem to be solved in a professional manner, I will provide adequate financial incentives to make the supplier accountable for their work. Someone willing to work for insignificant rates can walk away from a commitment whenever they like; there is nothing major riding on it for them. When someone's mortgage might be reliant on me settling their invoice promptly, I feel more reassured the job is going to get done. Keep this in mind when presenting your services to potential clients. The level at which you pitch your skills correlates with the opinion people form of you. So, if you are offering a low fee for a justifiable strategic reason, make certain your client understands that you never *usually* offer such low rates.

Do not fall into the trap of competing on price. When competing on price alone you will undoubtedly end up doing far more work than you are being paid for. When you set out to be the cheapest in the business or are willing to immediately drop your estimate to get the work, you will often attract the worst kind of clients. Decent clients—those deserving of hours of your time, who want the job done well—are not usually looking for the very cheapest estimate.

Worse still, competing on price is always a race to the bottom. Eventually someone is going to begin doing work below their cost price (and today, there are plenty of people out there who will buckle to the point of doing projects free of charge) and inevitably end up shutting the business or facing a tough struggle to ratchet their rate-card back up to realistic prices.

Establishing realistic pricing for your services and sticking to your rate-card is one of the best ways to keep your mind focused. You will avoid paying undue attention to low-end competitors, and it will force you to more carefully consider who you are pitching your business' services to. If you would never dream of getting out of bed for less than £10,000 (insert your chosen baseline price) then the people who charge a fraction of this are not in your orbit, they are not your competitors. There is no point comparing yourself to what the lowest end of the market is doing. Study what the very best are doing. How are they able to attract the types of clients happy to pay a premium for their services?

In summary

- Decide on your pricing structure and stick to it. It *is* okay to scale down a production and rethink areas of expense if a client needs to lower the budget, but *never* simply drop your estimate as a tactic to get awarded a project.
- Being passionate about projects is for amateurs, not for professionals. Never feel guilty about charging for work you enjoy doing, and be careful not to let enthusiasm for your work cloud your judgement when costing projects.

- Spreadsheets are your new best friend. Develop a costing sheet with enough flexibility to use for costing all varieties of production and implement it *every time* you cost a project.
- Brainstorming ideas, browsing for stock footage, or meeting with your client will all occupy time, and this time *will* have a *financial* cost associated with it. So, anything that occupies your time on a production must be represented on the spreadsheet.
- Does the client have the *resources* to pay *sensible* money? No matter how enthusiastic they might be, if they are aiming far beyond their means with an unrealistic or non-existent budget, the project is not going to happen.
- Do they have the *willingness* or *motivation* to pay? Some clients may regard video as a "nice to have" rather than a business essential. If the client lacks the motivation to act, the project will be forever on the backburner.
- Are both parties going to be getting a fair deal from this project? Will either one of you be compromising to an unacceptable degree just to get the job done?
- When costing a project remember that—unlike freelancing—you are not just covering your own salary. Your business has overheads, and *it* must also earn money and turn a profit.
- If the client is cagey about revealing their available budget, hint that you love when a client is open to trying exciting things; they will often reign you in.
- Never, never, work for free simply because the client has pushed you toward doing so or has dangled the carrot of lots of paying work in the future. If a client expects freebies, stand your ground—your businesses' time is billable.
- If you ever work pro bono, do it out of choice and for considered *strategic reasons*. The best reason is to prove you are capable of a style of work where you currently lack demonstrable experience. Before you begin work, get the client's assurance that you can use the video for promotional purposes, and ask them for a testimonial.
- Let the client know how much the no-fee project would have cost them at your usual rate. When the client does not have to pay, you might be able to gain some candid feedback from them about your pricing strategy.
- Do not fall into the trap of believing that demand for your pro bono offering is an indicator of a market clamouring for your work.
- If you are always busy—and you get commissioned without clients querying any aspects of your cost estimates—consider whether you might be underpricing your services.
- Your attitude to pricing sets the benchmark for your market positioning. Pricing will guide you toward who you market yourself to, and away from projects you are happy for someone else to take. Dropping your estimates to get work can cause you to lose faith in your offering, and drift toward the bottom end of the market.

12 The creative pitch

Why is it so important to deliver great pitches?

Pitching is the number one way you can demonstrate to a potential client that you have fully understood the objectives of their brief. A great pitch will demonstrate that you are on their wavelength, and that you thoroughly understand what they are trying to achieve. Your pitch will not only demonstrate the creative solutions you are proposing, it will also explore possibilities the prospective client might not have considered, and it will provide them a newfound enthusiasm for their project. A solid pitch will demonstrate that you have carefully considered their requirements and have developed suitable creative solutions that exceeded their expectations.

Creative flair aside, your pitch must also appeal to the client's cold corporate realities; it will demonstrate—with solid evidence—the *reasons* why you are sure your production will deliver value. The pitch will also present your cost estimates with transparency and clarity. Above all, a well-executed pitch demonstrates your abilities beyond the immediate project at hand. A great pitch will provide the assurance that you are well-organised, serious about winning, and committed to completing the project to the highest standard. Your pitch should embody the quality of the finished production you are proposing. A pitch is a hybrid of creativity, brand image, market positioning, logistics, financial data, and client relations. Getting all these elements to marry together into a cohesive and convincing argument is an artform. Deliver a great pitch, and you get paying work. Deliver a poor pitch, and all the hard work you did to get that client to the table will have amounted to nothing.

Don't make a pitch about you

Let us get one thing clear at the outset, pitches are *not about you!* One of the more common mistakes newbies—and even experienced production companies—make is to place the focus of pitches on themselves. They will open a pitch with an introduction about their business, their team, namedropping a few prestigious clients, the awards they have won, their guiding philosophy, yada, yada. Yawn. In some respects, being relatively new to the business can be beneficial. The more experience and credibility creatives gain, the more likely they are to get side-tracked into selling their past glories instead of trying to help their potential client. Corporate backstories are of limited interest to potential clients. After all, they have invited you to pitch creative solutions to them, so it would be safe to assume the hurdle of proving your credibility has already been cleared. Talking about yourself at length in a pitch is like peeing in a wetsuit; it gives you a nice warm feeling but leaves everyone else cold.

Search for brand guidelines, and follow them

Many brands publish guidelines for designers and agencies that detail exactly how to use their brand style, their colours, typefaces, and the tone-of-voice they use, i.e. the specific phrases and level of language the brand likes to use in its communications. Brand guidelines often show up—intentionally or unintentionally—on Google, and you can find them by simply searching for PDFs containing the brand's name suffixed with a handful of keywords such as "branding guidelines," "design guidelines," "tone-of-voice," "typefaces," etc. If you can't find their brand guidelines, get one of the free browser plugins (such as Fonts Ninja) to extract the names of typefaces, colour palettes, and even entire directories of images from the prospect's website and throw all of this information into a reference folder you can use to steer the design and tone of your pitch.

Franchises and global businesses (especially those licensing their brand to others) often have people on their teams whose sole job is to ensure third parties adhere to the brand guidelines. Get ahead of the game, demonstrate in your pitch that you know how to care for a brand identity. Show the potential client they can have confidence their brand will be presented correctly. If their guidelines specify their logo needs to have a set measurement of clear space around it, follow that rule. If their logo should never be overlaid on an image, do not do this in your pitch. Lastly, make sure you have not accidentally stretched or squeezed the client's logo. Short of spelling the name of the client's business wrong, adjusting the dimensions of their logo is the ultimate insult.

Your pitch is not only an opportunity to sell your creative solution to the prospect's problem (though this is of critical importance); the pitch is also a way to demonstrate that you "get" their way of doing things, you understand how to represent them, you feel their pain points, and your production will perfectly meet their requirements and the aspirations they have for their brand. Carefully implementing their choice of words, their weight of typeface, and accents of their brand colours creatively within your pitch is a subtle way to let them know they are in safe hands. Every pitch should not only sell your idea, but also demonstrate that you will be a good fit for them. When drafting a pitch that won us the work of a national retail chain, we gathered as much of their marketing literature as we were able to get our hands on.

We then went through it all with a highlighter to compile a dictionary of the type of words they frequently used to describe the ethos of their brand and their products.

Do some background research

If you are in the position of pitching to a high-profile (or long-established) business, there might be a greater amount of background information available to you. Sometimes the brief will not explicitly provide the entire backstory of the problem. Your potential client might be discussed in trade magazines, or by financial pundits. Recent industry news might also be pertinent to the pitch you are building. Do not try to be *too* smart with this though, you can risk making *assumptions* about matters where your potential client likely has far more context. But, sometimes, you might be able to find a problem they have not identified or feel uncomfortable being entirely candid about. At the very least, you will appear a little more knowledgeable about their area of business.

As an example, while pitching to produce the online marketing videos for a high-street retail chain we dug back through a decade of news and analysis within the client's sector. We discovered their brand had changed ownership several times, survived a public battering at the hands of some unflattering bad-press, and had spent several years maintaining a low-profile while re-cuperating and gathering its resources. The brief to us did not include any of this backstory. The brief simply wanted the videos to "raise the profile of the brand name among our target customer profile." So, forewarned by our background research, we were confident that pitching creative ideas with a grounding in "brand heritage" or "trust" were unlikely to hit the mark! Gaining some insight into your potential client's backstory, and their business sector, can be useful knowledge when assembling your pitch.

What should your pitch look like?

There is no single correct form for a pitch. After all, you are offering a very bespoke creative solution to your prospective client's problems. You do not want your pitch to feel like a generic template that you have padded out with a few specifics. Your pitch should feel coherent, entirely original, and carefully polished. The potential client should be able to see the careful consideration and expertise that has gone into its preparation. Word and PowerPoint are *not* design tools; it is best to avoid using them for page layouts. We design our pitches in Adobe InDesign, this is a professional page layout tool included with Adobe Creative Cloud. InDesign can create Interactive PDF documents allowing us to create a pitch presentation with clickable links to demos. Remember the old phrase "the way you do something, is the way you do anything," your pitch should be designed to a quality that gives a potential client an indication of the high standards you hold yourself to.

Let us get down to the two basic requirements where poor pitches fall short. A pitch must win two key arguments to stand any chance of working. Costs, logistics, and countless other elements can all be discussed and negotiated in more depth, but a pitch is dead in the water if either:

1 **The client is not able to *visualise* your creative approach**. You have not enabled them to *see*—in their mind's eye—how the final creation would look and function. In short, you have not successfully conveyed the idea from your mind to theirs. They just don't "get it."
2 **The client does not understand the *reasoning* behind the creative you are presenting**. They may well be able to *visualise* the ideas you have presented—they might even love the proposed treatment from an artistic perspective—but they are left struggling to understand how the production would fulfil the *objective* of their brief.

Solution: Allow the client to "see" the creative treatment by making it real

Creatives—filmmakers in particular—have the gift of being able to *think* in very vivid *visual* terms. We can look at a storyboard, or read a screenplay, and play the whole thing through in our minds. We have the knowledge and ability to visualise every camera angle, the pace, the flow, the music score. Our highly developed ability to visualise a finished production from mere written documentation and illustrations is a skill we might take for granted. We often assume someone else reading our pitches will be visualising—more or less—the same things as us.

You will often find yourself pitching scripts and storyboards to people with a less refined ability to visualise something conceptual. So, you need to give them a helping hand and make it "real" for them. We often accompany the printed scripts in our pitch with a fully mixed demo of a section of the soundtrack; hearing the style of voice and music we envisage will give the prospect an idea of how the track will sound. The printed script becomes audible. Fiverr is a great source for voice artists who can demo scripts inexpensively. To help the prospect understand how the visual elements of your concept will function you should consider creating what is known as an animatic. This is a video that uses images from your storyboard that are cut to the soundtrack. Again, this helps the prospect interpret how the concept will flow in its finished state. If you are presenting the creative for a production made only of graphics, produce a few seconds of video in the finished style so they can see exactly (more or less) what you will be making for them. Do everything you can to help them visualise what you are pitching to them. Despite the importance of helping them to visualise the creative solutions in your pitch, this is only half the battle. You also need them to understand *why* your creative is the *right* solution.

Solution: Prove the commercial logic by filling the gap in the client's knowledge

Creative people almost instinctively know when a creative solution will work. Less creative people need to see proof. Unfortunately, selling your idea on its creativity without explicitly making clear the rationale to justify your approach can make a client feel you have satisfied only your own agenda, and not theirs. The prospective client on the other side of the table—or looking at their webcam with indifference—likely has other things to deal with, and you might be the fourth producer who has pitched to them that day! It is usually not their job to keep their finger on the pulse of current video trends, or what plays well on social media these days. For your prospect to become enthusiastic about what you are pitching, they need to understand *how* to gauge if your solution is any good. Give them context. Demonstrate why it is the best course of action, and demonstrate why it is the *only* sensible course of action. Contrary to popular belief, clients really do want to commission original creative work, but it is the business advantages the production promises to bring about that will get them excited.

Presenting costs in your pitch

Never feel awkward about discussing the cost you present your pitch. There is a direct correlation between your feelings surrounding money and the confidence with which you can deliver your pitch, including the moment where cost is the topic of discussion. If you hold the unshakeable believe that the solutions you are presenting are worth every penny of your proposed budgets, do not skirt around the figures. The project costs what it costs, and it is delivering great value for money. Yet, I have been in several pitches where the creative solution has been presented, and the potential client then turns to the page outlining the budget. Silence. No one would say a thing. Several awkward seconds would pass while the client scanned the estimate. It is not a good approach, it makes the budget feel like a stumbling block, like the tense "speak now, or forever hold your piece" moment at a wedding. Present your prices with as much belief and professionalism as your creative solutions.

Get used to rejection

Okay, brace yourself. Behind every champagne-worthy win is a pile of dead pitches that somehow failed to make the grade. It does not matter whether you are new to the business, or a global agency with decades of experience, even a flawless pitch can meet a cold reception. We recently spent more than a week putting together a highly professional pitch for a video with a five-figure budget. Our pitch was rejected. We received the business equivalent of a Dear John letter, "The quality of proposals was so high, we struggled to make a decision, but unfortunately this time you were unsuccessful." Hey, it happens to us all!

Do not beat yourself up over rejections in competitive pitch scenarios. The odds will rarely be in your favour, and sometimes you will feel your time is being wasted, especially when you know for sure your pitch was the very best it could be. As Winston Churchill said, "Success consists of going from failure to failure without loss of enthusiasm."

Learn from your losses

Without wallowing in pity, it is good practice have a go at finding out what the winning producer did differently when answering the client's brief. Keep an eye open for the finished production, and remember that there's nothing to be lost by asking if the people you pitched to can find time to send a few pointers for what you might have done differently. Sometimes you will get nothing but stony silence, but other times you *will* get some useful information about what swayed the final decision in another producer's favour. Sometimes you will get the (slight) consolation that everyone had wanted to work with you but were vetoed by a single person higher up the organisation. In one instance we pitched for a television campaign and the CEO (who was not present during pitching) was forwarded all the competing proposals by the team we met. Against their team's recommendation, they took a strong liking to one of our competitor's concepts and—as the CEO had the final say—the decision was made without further debate.

File your pitch away and set to work on the next opportunity. Do not burn bridges or bemoan potential clients who "wouldn't know a good idea if it hit them in the face". On many occasions we have "lost" pitches and then had the prospect get in touch a year or two later to revisit our concepts. Maybe the production done by the winning producer did not quite deliver the objectives, or perhaps the chemistry of the working relationship wasn't right, maybe they opted for a "safer" idea at the time but kept ours in mind for further down the road. Often, it is simply the case that something at the client's end got derailed and the project was put on ice for a while. So, if they liked you on a personal level and you handled the rejection professionally, the potential client will feel the door is still open for them to get in touch again. You will be surprised how often this happens. On another occasion, our potential client went quiet for a couple of weeks after our pitch; we assumed they had awarded the job to another producer. Instead, they came back to us with a counterproposal; their team had been split evenly on who to work with and they really liked some of the examples in our reel, so they divided their budget into two smaller projects. They asked us to re-pitch (successfully) for one of the new projects that was most appropriate for our skills. A rejection is not always the final word, so it pays to always be magnanimous in defeat, because you may still get the last laugh.

Pitching in person

I suspect that more than a few producers walk into a meeting with a prospective client relatively unprepared. Merely being able to talk at length about yourself and the services you offer does not make you in any way prepared. You should treat every meeting—whether it is a "chemistry meeting" to get to know you, a briefing, or a pitch—as a big deal. Every in-person meeting is an opportunity for you to obtain paid work, and they all help to shape your reputation.

We prepare for many initial meetings by compiling a short dossier on the potential client and their needs: Who are we meeting? How did we initially connect with them? What do they already know about us? What do we already know about them? How large is their business? How long have they been established? Who are their clients? What impressions have we gained of their corporate culture? We plan our pitches down to details such as the journey time to reach their office, whether there is parking nearby, what we will be wearing, and what we need to take with us. Leave no stone unturned.

Don't let technology trip you up

Check what you need to bring to the pitch and ask how many people might be present at the meeting. Consider the best way to display your pitch and be prepared to have a solution to every potential hiccup. If you take along a presentation and examples of your work on a USB stick, make sure you have a copy of it all on the desktop of your own laptop or tablet. Always have a second memory stick to hand, because it is not at all unlikely that the client's computer will not play nicely with whatever you have brought along.

Never rely on your device being able to get onto the client's Wi-Fi to access additional examples of your work on YouTube or Vimeo. All elements of your presentation must always be saved in local folders. *Always.* I was told by a client that a competing production company who had met with them prior to us were unable to show any further examples of their work as they were not able to get their laptop to connect to the Wi-Fi. They lost the opportunity to impress the potential client because of their failure to anticipate a potential problem.

The client may have a beautifully installed corporate audio-visual system at their disposal, but always assume they do not, or that the person you are meeting may not know how to use it. You are supposed to be demonstrating that you are an unsurpassed expert in video production. So, fumbling around with remote controls and menus while trying to get your videos to play will not inspire a great deal of confidence in your professional abilities. Make sure you are slick!

Whatever media you have brought with you must have nothing other than your presentation materials on it; scrolling through dozens of other files to find the items you want to show doesn't convey the right image. Neither—in my opinion—does a cluttered desktop.

Make sure to carry a well-stocked *gadget bag* stuffed with an assortment of adapters and cables (kept tidy with Velcro loops) to connect to projectors or the large screens in client boardrooms. Little details like this do not go unnoticed. The simple fact that you planned and had brought both a five-metre digital and a five-metre analogue cable in your bag demonstrates that you are someone who anticipates the unexpected. Backup plans reassure potential clients.

In summary

- Always make sure your devices are fully charged and that you have all mains power cords to hand should they become necessary.
- Ask where you will be presenting and to whom. Knowing this will help you plan the best setup to make your pitch run smoothly.
- Gather everyone who will accompany you to the pitch and brief them thoroughly on the client, their requirements, and what has been discussed with them so far. If the pitch is more formal in nature, take the time to rehearse all the important elements even if you are going alone.
- Never go into a presentation without plenty of pre-planned fallbacks. Assume the scenario will be less than ideal: Your host has an awful computer, the projector is missing a cable, the host is not very technologically minded, and the IT person is out of the office. Always have a way to make things work. You can turn this to your advantage, coming across as an unflappable problem-solver.
- Do not have anything unrelated to the pitch on display, the same goes for any notepads or folders you have with you. Have a clean slate. You have arrived to give a potential client your entire focus. Do not bring all the administrative clutter from your desktop, or other clients, with you.
- Buy every imaginable cable, extender, and adapter you might need to connect your kit to whatever the client may provide at their office, and make sure you have it all to hand. If you want to be as neurotic as me, I recommend having a tick-box list prepared to check item by item that everything you could possibly need is packed and functioning.
- Pitches are make-or-break. If you win the pitch, you get the work. If the pitch does not meet the client's needs, it can be difficult to get a second chance—especially if the brief was competitive and other producers delivered more compelling pitches.
- Never make any pitch about you. Your backstory got you the brief. Now that you are in front of the client (either in person, or on a screen) make the pitch all about them.
- You have a visual mindset, you client might not. You must make your creative solution "real" for them. Create soundtracks and animatics, or render a short sequence of the finished piece. They must be able to visualise what you are pitching to them.
- Clients want to commission original creative work, but their overriding priority is that the production will deliver their objectives. Your

creativity will be regarded as self-serving if the client cannot understand how to gauge whether it is the right solution for *them*. Help them understand the *why* behind your creative.

- Gain a good understanding of your potential client's branding, colour palette, and tone-of-voice. They want to know you appreciate their branding, so that they can rely on you to produce work that will fit their image. Your pitch is the ideal place to demonstrate you care.
- When you use the potential client's logo, use it with respect. Poorly presenting their logo or brand name will bug them from the outset—so get it right.
- You will lose pitches. I lose pitches. The largest in the business lose pitches. Never get disheartened. You can do everything right, yet still lose—that is life. Find out if there was anything you could have done better, learn lessons if necessary, then get to work on the next opportunity.
- Even when you do not win the pitch, be so magnanimous in defeat that your prospective client will want to send you more briefs in future. Never burn bridges.
- Never stop trying to improve your pitching game, there is *always* more to learn about developing and delivering great pitches.

13 How to write an awesome script

I wrote at the outset that I would not be covering production techniques in any great depth, except for where the information might be beneficial to the overall operation of your business. Well, this is a part of the book where I *shall* allow myself to delve into an aspect of production the importance of which cannot be overstated. Scripts!

Your scripts are the vital blueprints from which all your productions are constructed. Poor corporate videos largely fall into one of two camps. On the one hand they are plodding, dull, and weighed down with superfluous minor details—they scream "made by committee." On the other hand, there are the videos stuffed with superficial hyperbole and corporate feelgood messages that add little substance; their remit seems to have been merely to add to a stockpile of generic marketing collateral. With the first variety of video, viewers are bored and overwhelmed by information overload. With the second variety, viewers learn nothing and are left wondering what purpose the video was meant to serve.

I have viewed countless corporate videos. Some of them were breathtaking, many others utterly awful. Yet, I do not often find fault with the quality of the cinematography, editing, or grading. Anyone can shoot stunning video on nothing more than a phone and edit their production on free software that used to be the preserve of feature film studios. Hence, the quality of *production* is often not where the flaws are found. What frequently separates amateurs from professionals is tight, energetic scripts that capture viewers' attention and tell a good story.

Think about this, how many Hollywood movies can you think of that have been a riotous success despite having an awful script?

Okay. That's a contentious question. You can likely name a few awful films that have somehow succeeded despite a flawed script, but they will be exceptions to the rule. Long story cut short: No amount of A-list acting talent, stunning computer graphics, or global marketing hype can drag a box office success out of the mire of a terribly written screenplay, mediocre dialogue, or an entirely flawed story concept. Failed movies can often be traced back to problematic scripts. Commercial video productions are no different.

Great scripts are answers to smart questions

I have observed that one of the significant factors that makes the difference between a humdrum video and an astounding one has been a script that has presented the information in an engaging and relevant way. The key questions we always ask while going through a client's brief—and any associated materials they have sent us—to draft a production script are these:

- What is the single most important message we must convey to the audience?
- How can we present this one message in the most simple and interesting way?
- What is superfluous, and might complicate the key message? Could this be cut entirely, or might it instead warrant its own video?
- Why would anyone viewing this video care in the slightest? How can we make it relevant to them?

If in doubt, cut it out!

The ideal script conveys just *one* key message, in *one* video, to *one* target audience.

Most scripts written for business videos fall short because the script has become bloated by an attempt to cover far too many objectives. Often, the producer has genuinely tried to do their job well but has had their arm forced by their client and has accommodated unnecessary additional material. In reality, it is not *always* going to be possible to achieve the "one message, one video, one audience" formula—it is an ideal—but even when you must achieve an all-encompassing production, you should always strive to remove clutter, allowing the key messages to remain clear.

Clients will often insist on the inclusion of in-depth descriptions of business processes or equipment. When writing the script, your task is to simplify their message, and that most often means cutting out anything which can more simply be demonstrated by the right shot, or the right graphics. Sometimes the client's industry terminology and abbreviations *will* have to be used. However, my rule of thumb is this: If an unbiased third-party from outside the client's industry sector were to view the video and find it largely incomprehensible, then your script is still far too heavy on dry terminology. Often, the very purpose a video is to create a more consumable "lite" version of a wooden PowerPoint presentation or lengthy official report in order to more widely disseminate the information to people within, or outside of the client's business. If you *can* simplify a laboured point, simplify it! If the answer to "Does this truly need to be in the script?" is "No"—cut it! I can—and often have—sliced overwritten scripts in half using those very criteria and lost nothing of importance.

The antidote to boredom

Is it possible to make interesting corporate videos about boring topics? Yes! This is an important creative skill, and it will give you a distinct competitive edge. Many of your clients will be all too aware that they are struggling to push a rock up a mountain in getting people to listen to what they have to say. If you have a magical way with words that can engage their audience, they will love you for it.

The formula to avoid writing a boring script is quite simple. Forget about the client's requirements, just for a moment. If you set about writing a script from the perspective of what your client wants to say to their audience, you are likely to convey the message in a stilted manner that won't resonate with viewers. Instead, approach your script from the perspective of a viewer. Reverse engineer the facts your client wishes to convey and turn them into questions the viewer would want to be answered. Figure out what questions a *viewer* would want to ask of your client. What was the most burning question *you* wanted answered when they were briefing you?

For example, let us say you have landed a major bank as a client (nicely done!). In a video for shareholders they want to make specific reference in the script to a ten-million-pound technology investment, because they feel it's an impressive number, because it's the largest amount they've ever spent, because that figure *means* something to *them*. So, including it in your script would be factually correct and give the client just what they asked for. However, I would argue many viewers would lack the context to appreciate whether presenting that ten-million-pound figure as a standalone fact is interesting information, or not. It is just not going to land with the exciting thump the client expects. Thinking about your script from a viewer's perspective might prompt a more relevant question the video should be answering, while still conveying the required information, "How many computers does a major bank own, and how much would it cost to replace every one of them?" Bingo. Lead with what a viewer would find interesting and weave the client's requirements through it. Far more interesting. Don't parrot dry facts, provide answers to intriguing questions.

Break with convention

Our client—a soft-furnishing retailer—would invite their store managers to an annual conference shortly before Christmas. At the conference they would unveil the year's sales figures, previews of new models and fabric patterns, store openings and upgrades, and the plans for their New Year Sale advertising campaign. All of this could easily run to a couple of days of stale PowerPoint presentations. Each year we were tasked with shoehorning all this information into a single 40- to 60-minute video production. Hour-long corporate videos are something of a rarity. Every year we had to devise a unique creative concept—brought to life with a great script—to convey a huge quantity of information in an entertaining manner. I cannot lie, it was far from an easy undertaking.

The retailer would have the managers in each division of their business send us their presentations, figures, and key announcements. It was mostly bland reporting and statistical data. It would have been easy to copy and paste most of this information into a script, put it on an autocue, and get the managers to read it to camera. The resulting video might have been marginally less fumbled and dry than a PowerPoint, but it would nonetheless become excruciatingly dull to watch after even just a few minutes.

So, we would continually devise creative new ways of presenting mundane corporate strategy in an endearing manner. Come late Autumn we would develop a theme for the conference, and the video would have to fit that theme. Each of our cast (the client's senior management team) was given a scene in which to star. We would sometimes bolster their performances with the inclusion of professional actors to keep their comically awful performances on track. Our crowning achievement was a version of Charles Dickens' *A Christmas Carol*, with the client's senior staff playing Scrooge, Bob Cratchit, and the three ghosts (each portraying three key parts of the retailer's focus for the year ahead). We shot the whole production at a Victorian working life museum with our cast dressed in period Dickensian costume. We had smoke machines, candles, open fires, falling snow, all the trappings of a period drama. The themed videos became an eagerly anticipated part of the annual conference.

Aside from being visually interesting—and often cringingly amusing—the success of those videos lay in scripts that had been trimmed and refined to hammer-home only the most pertinent messages in a memorable way.

So, if your client is willing to be daring, it is entirely possible to break with convention altogether.

Study the best writers—not just scriptwriters

How do you transform the dry information a client provides into a script with such precision and sharpness you could cut them with it?

Writing a script to explain, sell, or convince the viewer of a point of view is no different to any other type of creative writing. Learn from the lessons of the literary greats. Some of the most appropriate guidance comes from authors George Orwell and Stephen King. No doubt, they are very different authors, but they both provide similar advice to writers. I am reasonably sure Orwell never wrote a corporate video script or any advertising copy, but his pointers on writing read like a bullet-point list of how to get it right:

"Never use a long word where a short one will do."
"If it is possible to cut a word out, always cut it out."

"Never use the passive voice where you can use the active."
"Never use a foreign phrase, a scientific word, or a jargon word if you can think of an everyday English equivalent."

Stephen King expands on Orwell's one-liners. On the use of passive voice King says,

> Timid writers like passive verbs for the same reason that timid lovers like passive partners. The passive voice is safe. The timid fellow writes "The meeting will be held at seven o'clock" because that somehow says to him, 'Put it this way and people will believe you really know.' Purge this quisling thought! Don't be a muggle! Throw back your shoulders, stick out your chin, and put that meeting in charge! Write 'The meeting's at seven.' There, by God! Don't you feel better?

How does King's advice apply to drafting your scripts? Simple; writing in the active voice is more engaging and to the point; sentences are shorter and snappier. Writing in the passive voice sounds dull and contrived. For example, your client's first input for the script might read like this, "During the next twelve months we will be making a four million pound investment to enable the required improvements to be made to the dated IT infrastructure at the Lincoln call-centre." Sure, that conveys the *facts*. You *could* leave it as it is. But if the whole script is equally passive it will be a snooze-fest. Your job is to make this stuff better! If I had this script to edit, I would hack it down to size and address the viewer, "We heard your concerns, and that's why we are spending four million getting Lincoln's IT up to scratch!" It is far easier to achieve the active voice in your scripts when you write in the manner that people actually speak.

Stephen King's sage advice also comes into play when tackling descriptive writing. King says,

> The important part isn't writing enough, but limiting how much you say. — In many cases when a reader puts a story aside because it 'got boring,' the boredom arose because the writer grew enchanted with his powers of description and lost sight of his priority, which is to keep the ball rolling.

Corporate sales copy often indulges in flattering hyperbole, such is the nature of marketing literature. Borrowing wording directly from a client's marketing collateral without being selective can bloat a script with superfluous description.

Let's say you've captured a magnificent drone shot of a gigantic industrial facility. The shot just screams "this is the home of a major manufacturer." Question whether the script really needs to read "This is our gigantic ten-acre manufacturing site, and our largest facility here is the size of a forty-thousand seat football stadium." Does that description really add anything that the visuals alone do not already say by themselves? And will everyone viewing be able to grasp the extent of ten acres, or the capacity of a football stadium? Perhaps the footage alone says it all. Thankfully, commercial videos are not as rigid as a feature film or a drama, where a last-minute change of dialogue could cause a whole world of expensive implications! At the post-production stage, I have often removed lengthy sections of voiceover made redundant by a shot that has told a thousand words. Whether at the scripting stage—or making edits to the voiceover at the post-production stage—there's often little need to lay description on with a trowel. Less is more.

How will you know when you are on the right track with a script? *Read it aloud!* That is all you need do. I suspect many who have written a script for a video will not hear their words read aloud until the dialogue is recorded by a voice artist. When you read a script in your head it often flows well; you can scan read without having to take the breaths required to vocalise it. You will find out if a sentence is too long only if you speak it aloud!

Useful tip: Record yourself reading your script as a "guide track" to work with during the initial stages of production. Don't book your chosen voice artist until near the end of the project when the script and picture edit, or graphics, have been approved by the client. Voice artists are a friendly bunch, but they will have to charge additional fees if you keep asking them to record changes to the script.

In summary

- Scripts are the blueprints for your productions. A well-written script sets up a production for success.
- Improving your scriptwriting abilities is a competitive advantage. Clients need your skills to help them better explain something they are having difficulty communicating themselves.
- Overwritten scripts attempt to achieve too many goals or use too much technical jargon within one production. Underwritten or vague scripts (those padded with superficial hyperbole) usually lack a clearly defined objective or audience.
- An ideal script delivers just *one* message, in *one* production, to *one* audience. With skilled writing you can achieve a reasonable compromise; sometimes you have no option! But if the messages or audiences are too broad, or in conflict, it is likely that additional dedicated videos will better meet the client's objectives.
- Always question whether jargon or technical information is essential to a script. Simplifying convoluted language does not "dumb down" a script, it makes it more engaging. Avoid acronym overload.
- Using a script to simply convey facts from your client can make dull viewing. Flip your writing on its head, and approach your script from

the perspective of a viewer. Write your script in answer to questions that viewers would raise. What would the viewer find interesting about the topic? Present facts within an interesting context.

- Don't be a timid writer. Avoid writing scripts in the passive voice. Write in the active voice, use a little force, cut to the chase, and say it how it is!
- It may be tempting to copy and paste passages from the client's notes or marketing literature, but your script will flow far more elegantly if you work on a clean slate and write something fresh.
- You are writing for a visual medium, sometimes the pictures will say it all by themselves.
- The *only* way to know if spoken dialogue sounds good is to *read it aloud*. Reading aloud will highlight where your script is overwritten. If you have to take a breath where there isn't punctuation, it means your sentence is too long!
- Get your script locked (i.e. a high degree of certainty there will be no further changes) before booking your chosen voice artist.

14 Keeping your production organised

I shall begin this chapter with a few words of wisdom I often have cause to recall. Abraham Lincoln was quoted as saying "Give me six hours to chop down a tree and I will spend the first four sharpening the axe." Preparation is everything.

I remember a time before it was possible to edit an entire TV series at a leisurely pace on a laptop, in Starbucks. Videotape edit suites were seriously expensive, and we would book them by the hour at a post-production facility. Time was—quite literally—money. To prepare for an editing session we would watch through copies of the original camera rushes on VHS videocassettes, and do the edit "on paper" with a list of timecodes for direction during the edit. Enough with the nostalgia already! I was taught a vital skill: When you are working with billable time, be fastidious in your preparation and organisation.

Today, batteries last all day, memory cards allow for infinite shooting, non-linear editing allows (too many) mistakes to be solved, and our phones let us find quick workarounds to problems at a moment's notice. However, technology can provide so many safety nets and quick fixes that it can be tempting to relinquish some of our fastidious habits, and instead just "wing it."

If there is one crucial skill that ties together the smooth operation of your business, and the execution of well-oiled productions for paying clients, it is being scrupulously organised. Not just *regular* organised, but organised down to the very tiniest of minuscule details, making sure to factor every potential eventuality, every potential pitfall—however unlikely.

Nothing screams *amateur* quite like someone poorly prepared, regardless of how beautifully their production may turn out. Reading the testimonials our clients provide us, the common theme is not glowing accolades for the quality of our productions (but they are great, I assure you). Nope, most clients have praised our attention to methodical organisation and our ability to keep projects on track. It is like hiring contractors to renovate your home. No matter how good the quality of the contractors' work, or how reasonable their invoice, you will only recommend them to friends if they showed up when they promised, brought the correct materials and tools, and met the agreed deadline. Quality workmanship is expected by *default*, what sticks in the memory is how *smoothly* a job progressed.

For anyone on the receiving end of shoddy planning you would come across as highly irritating and, frankly, downright rude. Securing a positive reputation for being "a safe pair of hands" will become one of your most valuable assets. Pulling off a great piece of work in the end counts for little if concerns during production left the client with doubts about coming back for more, or a wariness to entrust you with more complex requirements.

We have recut countless hours of footage originally created by other production companies. The footage, or finished production, was sometimes exemplary. Yet, our client would frown when viewing it again, recounting a tale of a "really difficult shoot," or remarking that "it really did cost us a lot to put together in the end." Make sure that working with you always feels effortless. Your client needs to feel that everything has been taken care of and planned to a tee.

Forgetting to charge all the batteries, clear the memory cards, or check all the kit before you set off is amateurish. Not having the phone numbers of your clients and crew immediately to hand is amateurish. Not checking the weather, the catering arrangements, requirements for any necessary permits, the availability of power outlets, or enough parking spaces in advance of the shoot is—you guessed it—downright amateurish.

Okay, I think I have driven home the importance of planning. But do not forget to also keep your clients in the loop. Do they know the location of the shoot? Do they know what time they need to be there? Do they know they may need a change of clothes? Do they have your mobile number as well as your office number? Do they know how long they need to be in attendance? Of course, you have already asked about any food preferences or allergies, right?

When it comes to organising a production, there is no such thing as being over-prepared or too paranoid about checking you have got all the details covered. When everything goes right, your client will have had a pleasurable experience working with you. They will likely never consider how many variables you had anticipated and problems you had worked out in advance to keep things running smoothly.

Shooting schedule and shot list

In movies and entertainment, the shooting schedule is usually a mammoth document that marshals the whereabouts of hundreds of people across several filming units. The shot list (usually in the form of highly refined storyboards) will detail *thousands* of shots that need to be captured.

Thankfully—in commercial video projects—your crew will not often number double digits, and you will likely only have a few dozen setups to shoot in a day. However, it is *still* of paramount importance to have a list of exactly *what* needs to be filmed *where*, together with a schedule of the day. Whether you're filming a scene for a feature film, or a small product rotating on a turntable, you simply cannot arrive without a plan of action, and you must certainly *never* leave at the end of the day unsure as to whether you've captured all the material the client needs. In a 2001 Fast Company article, titled *Leadership Is Confusing as Hell*, Tom Peters stated,

> Leaders win through logistics. Vision, sure. Strategy, yes. But when you go to war, you need to have both toilet paper and bullets at the right place at the right time. In other words, you must win through superior logistics.

A video shoot isn't much different.

The best preventative measure to avoid a breakdown in your logistics is breathtaking in its elegance, and so simple that you can implement it on *every* project you will *ever* work on: **One sheet of A4 paper and a biro**.

Create a simple day-planner using a table with four columns. In the first (leftmost) column, break the hours of the day into equal segments heading down the vertical of the column. In the second column, insert the location you will be filming at any given time. For additional clarification, you should also include the name of the setup you will be shooting at the location. In the third column you will detail each shot you need to capture. In the fourth (rightmost) column add a checkbox that correlates with each of the shots you have listed. Strike-through each checkbox when you have captured a take you are satisfied with, then move on to setting up the next shot. You can scale this system to any size of production, but the overriding principle remains the same: If you religiously use a checklist on *every* shoot, you minimise the risk of forgetting a shot to practically zero.

The call sheet

Every shooting day is preceded by one simple document, the call sheet. This document lists all the information that everyone involved could need to know prior to the shoot. Its purpose is quite literally to get all the production team and contributors caught up on the same details. There are numerous call sheet templates available online, ranging from the most basic to those used for the shooting days of feature films. For most corporate work, the simplest template will do the job. A single page can cover all the details below:

Your office and mobile contact numbers

Because you should be the one person who can give definitive answers to everything.

The names of the clients and crew, and their contact numbers

Some clients may require all this information to be provided in advance as a health and safety requirement (a shoot at an industrial plant, for example) so it is best to begin compiling all of this information as soon as you have got people committed to working on the project.

The time that everyone needs to convene for the day ahead

Always factor 30–45 minutes of contingency at the very least. If everyone arrives on time you will be able to unpack at leisure and have a tea while running through the day ahead. If someone gets delayed because of traffic they might miss out on a morning drink, but the shoot should otherwise be able to begin on schedule.

Where and when to rendezvous

Usually this will be the location of the shoot. But if it is a long journey to the location then your meeting place may be a hotel the night before, this also needs to be on your call sheet. Always include the full address, postcode, and the most appropriate phone number for every location.

Directions to the location and details of where to park vehicles

Map apps might only get people in the vicinity of where they need to be. It can often be difficult to locate a specific reception area, manufacturing line, or industrial unit on a large commercial site. If the location is potentially difficult to find, take a Google street view screenshot, or even ask the client to send you a photo or a description of your rendezvous point, and use the call sheet to make sure everyone has those same directions, e.g. would the "East Gate" be easily recognisable to members of your team who have not previously visited? Ideally you will have visited in advance to check out the parking situation, and agreed the number of vehicles your team will be arriving in.

At a time long before smartphones I worked with someone new to planning shoots. Our filming location appeared to be a prestigious—easy to locate—address in central London, named something like the "European Medical Institution" and the name of the nearest tube station. We disembarked lugging cameras and tripods, and wandered around the nearby streets to find a large building with a big brass plaque befitting the name of the client. After half an hour of searching we resorted to asking in local shops if they knew where the place was. Eventually we phoned a colleague and got them to search for the full address. The "Institution" was the name of the gathering of people we had been booked to film; the location was simply a hired room in a conference centre opposite the tube station. Thankfully, the time contingency *had* been planned correctly and we managed to set up with time to spare. Lesson learned: If any detail of the call sheet *could* be misunderstood—or left open to interpretation—assume that it *will be* and fill in the blanks.

Special requirements

Highlight anything your client specifically requires of your team, and anything else you think will make the crew's day easier. In hazardous environments your client will supply items like ear defenders and safety glasses for visitors, but they will often make recommendations against loose-fitting clothes or trainers. Make sure this is passed on and understood by the crew.

In other situations, the requirements are just basic common sense, but highlight any practicalities that may need addressing. For instance, if you are filming at a nature reserve or a farm make a note in the call sheet that your crew should bring suitable footwear, wet-weather clothes, etc. Film crews are a very pragmatic and well-travelled bunch, and they have usually considered such practical requirements from the outset—but a heads-up on the call sheet is good practice. I recall a shoot for a TV commercial that took place in a meadow at the height of a very hot summer. One of the runners had forgotten both antihistamine for his hay fever and high-factor sunblock, so he had to leave us for almost an hour to go find a supermarket.

Wrap time

State the time you intend the filming day to finish but make clear it is a calculated estimate and not truly definitive. For the sake of ongoing goodwill—and unplanned expense—never simply pluck an unrealistic time out of the air and risk overshooting it by a mile. Production crews are no strangers to long days, but do not take advantage. Professionals create realistic schedules and do everything they can to stick to them, often managing to get everyone packed and heading home at near-enough the estimated wrap time. It is not unheard of for profit margins on projects to have been eroded by overtime charges levied by a crew who felt they had been taken advantage of by an ill-prepared production company. Make the day run on-schedule, and your crew's invoices will not have any unpleasant extras.

Health and safety

A health and safety risk assessment should be conducted for every production. Although a risk assessment is not strictly a requirement for inclusion on a call sheet, it can be a wise precaution to add any pertinent details from risk assessments to your call sheets. After all, not many events will cause you to lose a client permanently quite so efficiently as inadvertently injuring or killing them.

Okay, I leapt directly to the worst possible scenario there. That said, as the production company, it will be *your* responsibility to make sure your crew and clients are always working in safety. Unless you are using stunt performers or pyrotechnics (and if you are, I would love to know more about your clients) your health and safety considerations are likely to be quite straightforward, though no less important. You do not need to be qualified to conduct a risk assessment; you just need to be a competent human being with ample common sense. During production planning you should always visit your filming location to conduct a "technical recce" (reconnaissance) to establish camera positions, lighting requirements, the location of power outlets, etc. During your recce you should also conduct a risk assessment, listing all the hazards with the potential to strike on the day of filming. You will need to list all the common considerations that are true of any shoot—such as trailing cables and manual handling of heavy items—but also identify less obvious hazards specific to the location or the nature of what you're filming. For example, on the technical recce of a woodland clearing we found a broken bottle, so we noted on the risk assessment that the crew beware of the possibility of broken glass at the location.

Alongside the risks, you must note the measures you are putting in place to minimise the potential for harm, both against specified dangers and the more general precautions you are putting in place. Your risk assessment should let your crew know the location of the First Aid kit, and who the First Aider is. If you do not have one, take a First Aid course! You should also check where the nearest Accident and Emergency is located and add its location to your risk assessment. That may sound melodramatic, but small accidents can happen. We had to take a production runner for treatment when they trapped a finger in the lid of a flight case. I get it, all of this must sound like needless additional planning and doom mongering when you are simply filming a piece to camera, but when you use a familiar template it is not an onerous task.

If you find yourself working for a client with operational hazards that might not be immediately apparent to you, they will most often conduct a specialist risk assessment on your behalf. It is likely they will also provide the necessary training and provide a chaperone on the shoot to act as a safety advisor. Comply unwaveringly with everything they tell you to do, they will not work with you again if your shoot causes them unnecessary headaches.

Packing for maximum efficiency

Getting your organisational skills up to scratch should include your attitude to packing and transporting equipment. Work just once with someone who does not appreciate the importance of a careful packing routine, and you might come close to understanding the blood-boiling frustration I feel when kit is poorly arranged, difficult to locate, or simply missing altogether!

Keeping equipment properly maintained, methodically organised, and thoroughly checked before each shoot—especially if you are using rental kit—is one of the hallmarks of an efficient professional. Plus, it will save you the major headache of showing up at a location with flat batteries, full memory cards, or a crucial bit missing from something. The importance of keeping kit organised becomes more critical as your projects increase in complexity. Our production team even carries a toolbox with such varied items as fishing wire, bulldog clips, cables ties, Blu-tack, scissors, masking tape, and essentials like a selection of small screwdrivers and Allen keys. It is easy to gradually accumulate a substantial quantity of essential bits and pieces, but it is all of little use if you can't find it when you need it.

Becoming obsessive about the organisation of production equipment not only allows you to sleep soundly the night before a shoot, it can also instil your client with greater confidence. No matter what the demands of the day, you—or any member of your team—will have the satisfaction of being able to immediately lay hands on the required gadget or gizmo. I have attended several shoots where a missing widget or dooh-dah has required a trek back to the crew vehicle to rummage through bags or jacket pockets. On a day with a tight schedule, crucial minutes can be wasted just looking for stuff.

The number one rule for never losing items: Everything has its place. Every item of your kit must have a dedicated home to where it is always returned. At any point during a shoot you should be able to grab what you need without having to think where it might be. When you've *really* nailed down the *logic* behind your packing system, even crew you have not worked with before can instinctively reach for what they need from your bags and cases.

Not only does a thoroughly organised packing system make for a swift de-rig after a shoot, it also minimises your chances of leaving anything behind. If you know where something should always be kept, you will immediately be able to question its whereabouts when you spot an empty space in a case.

How do we organise everything we take on location?

For starters, buy decent bags and cases. Professional equipment cases aren't cheap; for instance, the world-renowned Pelicase brand is popular with film-makers and the military alike. There's good reason why many of the free-lancers we work with have kept the same cases for many years: They have travelled the world, and they are still in one piece! From experience, a robust backpack is also handy (ideally one designed for photographers, with rigid internal compartments) as there often are not enough hands to carry all the cases! If you do have to leave a lot of kit in the vehicle and the location is some distance from the parking, a backpack can be a perfect place to stash documents, spare batteries, and small bits of sound kit. I have purchased cheaper copies of the pro-gear, and they have all prematurely given up, coming unstitched or suffering from broken zips or snapped plastic clasps. If you have kit that goes out on the road frequently, invest in tried-and-trusted brand name bags and cases.

I've worked with crews who have used large adhesive vinyl numbers (the type you might use to apply your house number to your garbage bins or mailbox) and developed a shorthand for knowing where things are, "Laura, can you pass me case three?" We use a similar simple system; sticking fluorescent camera tape to the cases and using a marker pen or Sharpie to spell out exactly what the case contains. Batteries live in the case labelled "BATTERIES" and cables, unsurprisingly, reside in the case bearing the huge label "CABLES." This clarity can be helpful when it comes to packing up swiftly at the end of a shoot, anyone on the crew can identify where stuff should be returned to. Simplicity removes a great deal of room for error.

In summary

- It is your production, so it is your responsibility to keep it progressing smoothly.
- Anticipate all the things that could go wrong and ensure they don't!
- There is an old military maxim, "Slow is smooth, and smooth is fast." Whether the project in hand is a short motion-graphics piece, or a complex shoot spanning a dozen locations, you should always invest plenty of time upfront for careful planning. Never wing anything, be fastidious in keeping your projects organised. When you have planned a project well, the creative elements of your production will flow more smoothly.
- No matter how stunning your creative artistry, commercial clients will be paying attention to how professionally you manage their project. Thorough planning—having everything under control—demonstrates to clients that their project is in safe hands.
- If any part of your planning will impact on the client's movements or decisions, do not assume all will be okay on the day they need to be involved.
- When your project involves filming, you must draw up a call sheet. This document will squash any assumptions your client or crew might be tempted to make about the day of the shoot and, quite literally, get everyone on the same page. It is a non-optional document.
- Risk assessments are not difficult, you must risk assess even the most simple of shoots—and use the call sheet to syndicate information about potential hazards, and the precautions that are being taken, to everyone who will be present.
- Strive to become irritatingly pedantic about packing equipment—whether your own, or not—with military precision. Not only will you be able to grab what you need at a moment's notice, you will also lessen your chances of losing something, especially important when you are using someone else's kit.

15 Coaching on-camera contributors

You are probably thinking, "Why would I need to know about performance coaching or conducting on-camera interviews? I just want to run a production company!" Okay, you might be able to dodge this responsibility. However, if you find yourself regularly producing video for internal corporate use (for management to communicate to their staff) you will inevitably be called on to direct on-camera performances; most often because no one else is available to do it.

Using a professional presenter

Many personalities, and TV journalists specialising in your client's sector of business, are freelance talent and will be available for corporate work. We have used several celebrity presenters, and even national primetime newsreaders, for both public marketing videos and internal staff productions. They can raise what may otherwise have been a humdrum video (especially those covering in-depth or less-than-exciting subject matter) to something that feels closer to mainstream TV. If the budget is reasonable, and the complexity of the subject matter would benefit from an experienced speaker, enquire with the agents of suitable presenters. Agents usually reply quickly either to politely decline or to open negotiations about the scope of the project and the fees. An experienced presenter with a track record of work in your client's sector can greatly raise the credibility of your production and make the shoot more straightforward.

Coaching and directing contributors

However, you will usually not have the luxury of an experienced interviewer or presenter to take care of on-camera dialogue. You will have to go it alone when an interview is required. Let's say you're shooting at a tradeshow where exhibitors or visitors need to be called on to contribute something insightful with only a few moments' notice, someone is going to have to ask the questions. In the absence of your client stepping-up to do the job of interviewer, it's most likely going to fall to you or someone on your crew to ask some probing questions, and steer the interview towards gaining something of value to your client. The same is true if you must interview your client on camera.

I attended a scientific expo where a new medical technology was being unveiled. Our client was exhibiting at the expo and at the eleventh hour they decided it would be an ideal setting to explain the commercial implications of their technology on-camera, creating a short promotional video to release after the expo. With almost no time to plan ahead, we arrived an hour ahead of the doors opening to grab a coffee and a breakfast muffin or two (always take advantage of a free buffet) and sit down with the client, warm them up a bit, and note down bullet points of things they needed us to capture on camera. The team running the exhibition stand were the very scientists who had developed the technology. Brilliant! The information was going to come straight from the horse's mouth, so to speak. It was immediately clear they were all talented geniuses who would be able to hold exceptionally detailed discussions with other scientists attending the expo. However, the brilliant scientists were most definitely *not* marketing professionals. It was clear they were going to struggle to find words to simplify their tech in terms that people viewing the finished piece would be able to grasp.

You will have to coach interviewees who were often told only at the last moment they needed to speak and are not sure what is required of them. The most common problem: Your interviewee will be some type of specialist, and specialists often use shorthand only other specialists can decipher. A detailed technical discussion is not always what the people commissioning the production require. That said, do not just *assume* the language needs to be "dumbed-down," ask the client what level of familiarity and understanding the viewers are likely to have of the topic at hand. For several years we produced videos for an engineering company. To this day I have little understanding of the terminology they preferred to use in their productions, seemingly the more complex the better. Yet, they were always satisfied with the results. So, bear in mind that not all clients will be looking for snappy soundbites.

Anyway, I jumped off course. Let me get back to that scientific expo! It was clear the technical experts needed coaching to crank up their energy level. They needed to *sell* their technology in a way the target audience would be able to understand. To coach a client effectively, you need to understand what they are trying to convey. While the scientists continued to set up for the day ahead, we took a handful of their promotional literature to speed-read and pick out the most pertinent sales messages, adding them to a bullet point list. The list would help us to keep the interviewees on track, and prompt them to recount relevant information.

Staying clear and concise

Having read through the literature for the product we were aware it could create a major speed-boost for medical diagnostics, which could save buyers' money in the long-term. So, I led with the question "What are the drawbacks of the current technology, and what kind of speed increases could users expect from your new system?" The answer was okay, but *only okay*. So, I underlined the question on my pad and made a mental note to return to it later. It is almost always the case that an interviewee gets more comfortable as an interview progresses. So, when the interview is drawing towards a close, say—with great enthusiasm—something like "This has been great, really wonderful stuff, but now that you're on a roll could we look at those first couple of questions again?" If you need to, remind them of the gist of the answers they gave; refining a little if you felt they were too lengthy first time around. Interviewees will often give more concise and snappy answers to questions the second time around, having gathered their thoughts and realised they may have added some unnecessary padding first time round. In the edit, this means you can launch into their piece with a striking, succinct, statement—captured when they were operating at full power!

Be wary of trying to put the client's exact choice of words in your interviewee's mouth. Some clients get nervous that anyone appearing on camera for their video might say the "wrong" thing, and so, to some extent, they will want to dictate what interviewees say. I have not experienced this being done in a manipulative or misleading way, but the client would sometimes have conjured up a smart-sounding way of conveying some thought and would try to get the interviewee to repeat it word-perfect. We have always tried to shoot these to satisfy the client, but—reaching far back into the crevices of my mind—the "scripted response" takes have usually *not* made the final cut. Most people will struggle to repeat verbatim even something they have only just heard. Trying to recall exact words will trip them up. The same is true of cue cards and any other off-camera prompts. Their use will draw your interviewee's eyes away from where they should be and will cause a wooden and unnatural delivery. It is always possible to spot when someone is reading from notes. Instead, give them an example of the direction they might take when answering, and let them know it will be absolutely fine for them to say it in their own words, and they really *must* use their own words—albeit coached for maximum impact—otherwise the piece can come across like a rehearsed political soundbite. You know the type of interview, the politician has been briefed on the exact wording of every answer. The interview is so rehearsed that they frequently get stuck in a loop of repeating the same sentences again and again to prevent themselves getting drawn away from providing the scripted responses. Parroting of another person's words in an interview is something we are all accustomed to noticing. The more casual and conversational you can make an interview, the more pleasing the finished result.

Getting a nervous interviewee to chill

Sometimes an interviewee is—to use one of my favourite expressions—"bricking it." Mark Twain is credited as having said, "There are two types of speakers: Those who get nervous and those who are liars." Getting an on-camera contributor to appear at ease when they might be anything but will require patience, empathy, and just a little understanding of psychology. Whatever tactics you bring into play, the calm you exude as a producer/ interviewer is infectious. Remind your contributor that no one's in any hurry, and they have all the time in the world to get to a point where they are happy with the outcome.

Jonny Baker is a Personal Speaking Coach at The Challenge, London,

> My number-one rule is to be to put yourself at ease. We naturally pick up on others' emotional states, often without realising it, and take our cues from whoever is controlling the situation (the interviewer). You cannot put someone else at ease without first being at ease yourself and if you add your concerns to the speaker's already present nervousness, they get confirmation of their nervousness. Then you have a far greater challenge on your hands! That is not to say you should ignore your speaker's nervous behaviour—remain aware—just edit your own response. Make a choice to believe in them and their ability to communicate powerfully, respond with empathy and rock-solid determination that there is a top-level performer inside them. There are other things you may do in addition to this, but they won't make much of a difference, unless you are first at ease and confident about your speaker.

If the interviewee's enthusiasm seems to be on the wane or their confidence is beginning to slip, step up your coaching even further! Never allow themselves to beat themselves up over fluffing their words or needing several takes to reach the "perfect" answer you have all been holding out for. Lyn Roseaman of *Now You're Talking* is a public speaking coach with more than 25 years' experience,

> For some people, every take brings additional pressure that can affect their ability to focus. This in turn causes more mistakes and the need for more takes. The 'Take-Mistake' cycle is pernicious. The more takes they do, the more anxious they become, the more mistakes they make. And to top it all, just as they're almost at the end, they fluff their words or completely forget what they wanted to say.

Lyn recommends that speakers who feel themselves getting into the "Take-Mistake" cycle allow themselves to take a break and grab a refreshment. Falling blood-sugar levels and dehydration can cause brain-fog and irritability, sometimes just taking five minutes for a drink and a snack can get things back on course. Lyn recommends production teams should actively let anyone appearing on camera know that it's fine to ask for a filming break to gather their thoughts. Her advice for an interviewee, "Don't be afraid to ask the crew for a short time-out. Chances are everyone will appreciate you taking the lead, rather than worrying about how to take a break without offending you. Break the 'Take-Mistake' cycle—Break. Revive. Retake."

Lyn's advice tallies with my observations. We spent more than a decade patiently coaching a single client. This was a very senior individual who—because of their position in the business—had no option but to frequently show their face and "address the troops" as it were, even though they were far from a natural speaker. On-camera they always struggled to get their words straight, and the first time we worked with them we shot an hour of material to get just a couple of minutes of coherent delivery. It was painful, but we remained unflappable and encouraging even though the executive was getting tired and very flustered that they could not quite convey their message. We steadily worked with them until we got a take (the best we could) that we all felt hit the right note. Our patience was rewarded, we had put them at ease and captured the message they wanted to get out to their staff. We went on to have a very long working relationship, and we continued to quietly factor additional time into our schedule when working with them, and always had notes prepared to help keep them on track. One other trick we kept up our sleeve was to find a need to alter a light, or change battery on the camera (regardless of whether it was really necessary) and let the executive know they could stand down and take a five-minute breather, blissfully unaware the break in recording was really for their benefit. With many successful projects behind us, the executive eventually became a one-take soundbite-delivering machine; well, *almost!* Jonny Baker has picked up on a similar vibe from the many speakers he has coached,

> Part of your speaker's frustration may well be the expectation and pressure they feel coming from the interviewer and production crew to deliver their best performance in a limited amount of time. Reflection, patience, perseverance, and belief in your speaker will get them a long way! However, if your speaker is stuck in a downward spiral, regardless of your own at-ease-ness, don't pretend to have all the answers. Why not ask your speaker what they would need to do, change, or have, to begin to reignite their enthusiasm? Then work together to achieve this. No one else knows their emotional state and needs as they do.

Jonny also uses the intriguing approach of grasping the nettle with both hands, and addressing the interviewee's feelings directly,

> You can get them to talk openly about how they feel to the camera (or indeed, off camera), how they feel about speaking on camera; and how they feel about the message they want to deliver. They are likely to communicate two contrasting feelings, gaining an opportunity to reconnect with their purpose and passion. Listen carefully and home in on any emotions they do express, asking further questions to expand that emotion.

I can see this approach working well when there is plenty of time beforehand to talk through what the interviewee wants to achieve from their piece, especially when coaching them to deliver something longer than just a couple of soundbites. My rule of thumb has always been to get chatting to on-camera contributors as early as possible on the day of the shoot to build rapport. It is even better if you can get to know them and brief them on what is required the day before.

Kicking life into dull speakers (*not* "kicking" in a *literal* sense)

Unless highly practised or trained, not many people possess the ability to switch on instant power and charisma when seated in front of a camera. Yet, for your production, they are usually the best-qualified—or indeed the *only*—person who can speak with authority on the subject at hand. I have witnessed an odd phenomenon when getting people ready to appear on camera. We would have a coffee with them before filming and discuss what points we needed to cover in the interview; they would enthusiastically and casually recite all their expertise without hesitation. We would sit them down in front of the camera and the enthusiasm we had just witnessed would vanish. They would slow their speech, lose the natural highs and lows in their delivery, and almost turn into a completely different person. I recall one guy we interviewed at a manufacturing plant, off-camera he was beaming with pride at the efficiency of their new method of operation; boastful phrases like "truly revolutionary" and "like nothing else in the industry." Great stuff! When asked about this new method on-camera he stood motionless, unblinking, and delivered a monologue of dry statistics to the lens. We got the guy amped-up again, but it is not at all uncommon for people to radically adjust their natural speech delivery when a camera is on them.

I have found one of the easiest, and most reliable, ways to get an interviewee in the flow of talking with enthusiasm is to take a genuine interest in their business and what they are trying to achieve. Get on board with their goals and help them find ways to express those goals. I have long been fascinated by problem-solving and the operations of business; luckily for me that is what a lot of corporate videos are about. When you get to go behind-the-scenes of any business, you will have all kinds of questions you would love to have answered. Getting your interviewee to satisfy your curiosity quickly puts them at ease, they will be on safe ground answering questions in their area of expertise. One of the earliest projects I worked on was for a manufacturer of combine harvesters. These agricultural monsters were vivid green in colour. Out of genuine interest, I asked whether the mechanics under the hood were also the same colour. Turns out, they *are* the same intense green shade on the inside, and it is an exceptionally hard-wearing paint that must comply with all kinds of regulations to ensure it does not end up in the food chain. The client was on a roll enthusing about the superior specifications of their product, clearly delighted that I was interested. If you really want to raise an interviewee's level of enthusiasm, buy their product! Though, you can stop short of buying a combine harvester.

In summary

- Consider a professional presenter if the client's budget can stretch. A professional speaker can be transformative, especially when a complicated message must be conveyed clearly or with additional gravitas.
- Always be ready to step into the role of interviewer because it *is* going to happen.
- Regular people—when put forward to speak on camera by their boss—have often not been given details as to what is required of them, or what they are "supposed" to say. You will have to brief them and be their coach.
- Keep in mind where the viewer is at; are they a fellow specialist who will understand technical jargon, or do you need to brief your interviewee to give a marketing-friendly soundbite?
- Make sure you understand what the client hopes to achieve by including interviews or soundbites in the video. It is essential to know the intended outcome so that you can ask the right questions to get there.
- Let your interviewee get in their stride and answer all your questions. When they're comfortable and warmed-up, take them back to the first couple of questions. They're going to be more concise and less hesitant second time around.
- Avoid letting your client dictate word-for-word what they hope the interviewee will say, even if the interviewee is one of their own members of staff. Simply ask the right questions to reach the answer in the interviewee's own words.
- If a speaker absolutely must deliver something to camera that is word-perfect, use a teleprompter. They are not expensive, and they will save a *lot* of time. Cue cards or notes will draw a speaker's eyeline away from the camera and create a wooden performance.
- Never infer that you are working to a deadline or are running late. Never make an interviewee feel under pressure. Reassure your interviewee that you have all the time in the world, and you want to make sure they are happy with their contribution.
- If you are at ease, it will help put your client and the interviewee at ease. Even on the 30th take, you should still appear calm and encouraging. Of course, in your mind you are screaming into a pillow. But you *know* they *can* deliver a great soundbite!
- Offer your interviewee a small break to gather their thoughts. If you feel they could be rattled by the suggestion of taking a break, find a reason

to conveniently pause for "technical reasons" and stand them down for five minutes.

- Ask the person appearing on camera what they really want to convey and help them find a straightforward way of saying it in a *concise* statement. Speakers very often trip themselves up by not knowing when to *stop* talking.
- Let the contributor know they do not need to "perform" in any way, they can be themselves and speak exactly as they would if the camera were not present.
- Ask the contributor a few questions that personally intrigue you, or where you know their answer will play to their specialism or area of interest. Their answers might not be required by the project, but genuine unscripted questions can be answered in a conversational way, without pressure on them to deliver an "on message" answer.

16 Communicating with your clients

Establish the level of client involvement

Most of your clients will be a pleasure to work with, enthusiastically collaborating with you throughout production. For some clients, being involved in the production of a video is a welcome change of scenery and something they will enjoy working on. Other clients will be busy with more pressing matters and will keep their distance from the project they commissioned; to them it is not a novelty, just another cost of doing business. Depending on your personal working style, you might find the boundless enthusiasm of first type of client a little intrusive at times, they might offer spontaneous suggestions that could lead a project off course, or invite themselves to sit-in on edit sessions. Whereas the second type of client can be difficult to reach when queries arise or might delegate responsibility for a project mid-production. Remain flexible and accommodate the client's preferred manner of working, there is no single "correct" way. Learn how they prefer to work and adapt your relationship to suit. You will need to apply a different style of relationship management to each client.

Strive for clarity in everything you say

Your client interaction will benefit from the daily application of the same principles of the business you are in: Clear, specific, and accurate communication. A general rule of both life and business is this: Mistakes are often caused because someone along the line had not been in possession of the right information at the right time, had not been kept in the loop, or had simply remained silent when they should have spoken-up.

I am sure you know someone who sends emails that needlessly ramble on for a couple of pages. Despite the enormous wordcounts, their messages will provide only vague guidance in a noncommittal fashion, leaving you none the wiser for the several minutes you took to read it. Years ago, I had a client who would dispatch instructions from their Blackberry the moment a thought began to take shape in their mind. At all hours of day and night I would receive a stream of cryptic and sometimes conflicting instructions.

Oddly, even where something appeared to be a firm request the sentence might sometimes be closed with a string of question marks, leaving me in limbo until I was able to get hold of them on the phone. Some clients might not be the clearest of communicators, so you will have to pick up the slack—you must *always* strive to maintain clarity in your interactions with them.

Your replies to client queries should always be precise. Leave no room for ambiguity or confusion. Provide clear statements as to what your next course of action will be, and when the action will be completed. Include firm dates and times if you can. I am a great exponent of formatting emails with numbered lists and bullet points; I will sometimes attach a clearly structured and formatted PDF wherever the complexity of the project warrants this level of detail.

My method of working—making sure that nothing falls through the cracks—usually involves breaking any task into individual subtasks that I can strike off my list as they are completed. Here is a pro-tip when it comes to list-making: Ensure that any task on your list is a specific and well-defined *action*, and *not* merely an intended *outcome*. If items on your list look like nebulous vague hopes for the future, they are likely not easily actionnable.

When your client works by committee

It is inevitable that you will have the somewhat dubious "pleasure" of working with an organisation run by committee. Clients who must make decisions by committee, or via extended ranks of management, will often require you to modify your methods of working to keep projects running smoothly.

When dealing with larger organisations—especially those in government or a regulated industry—you will rarely be taking instructions or receiving feedback from just one individual. You will have to accommodate the views of multiple departments, each evaluating a project from a different viewpoint. To further complicate things, individuals may not be in the same office, or even the same country. One or two of them will inevitably be away on holiday during the project and unable to be fully involved. On their return they might be irritated they were not kept in the loop and will set about raking through decisions made in their absence. The email chains get lengthy as even simple queries are referred through the ranks and disseminated far and wide, ensuring no one on the committee can complain of not being consulted. Decisions will often be further delayed when a handful of people can't be contacted for one reason or another, "David really has to sign-off on this too, but he's at a conference in Norway. He's told me he will have a look at the clips you've sent over and get back to us all with his thoughts in a few days." And progress comes to a halt for a while.

Working by committee may sound horrendous. That said, this can be the standard way that large enterprises function. However, you can turn committee and wide reach working to your advantage. Simply keep as much of the "leg work" on a project off of the client's action list. Keep them updated and in the loop, but do not burden them with having to make unnecessary decisions.

- At the outset ask your client how it is best to communicate with them. Does all communication need to go through a single person acting as a coordinator, or is it okay to use CC'd emails, or a weekly Zoom call to keep everyone in the loop?
- If the project is likely to be unusually complex—or a prolonged commitment—ask whether an online collaboration and approvals process could help keep operations running smoothly. For several of our clients we maintain a shared Dropbox folder to keep our project files in sync with theirs. There are countless other cloud-based tools available for more complex collaborative project management and group chat tools—Microsoft Teams, Asana, Workfront, Trello, Twist, Smartsheet, Vimeo Business, and Google Teams (and by the time of publication, likely many more!).
- Being organised is essential but do be wary of over-complicating, especially if your client is not overly comfortable with technology. I have worked on some major projects through the years, and for the most part the clients would not have appreciated the additional headache of having to learn a new way of working. If your client would rather navigate a project with phone calls or emails, do not force your preferred way of working on them.
- Ascertain the hierarchy within the client's organisation. Who gives the final say on any given matter? Should you action any requests before waiting for an "okay" from someone else? This is something you will learn over a period. Quite often you'll need to work on a few projects with a client before you become familiar with the subtle nuances of whose word carries the most weight; you can't really ask "Do you actually have the authority to sign-off on this alteration?" By a process of elimination, you will begin to appreciate who has the genuine authority to make changes to an ongoing project.
- Will all the decision-makers be in the loop from the outset, or will final approval rest with someone else? Often our completed productions have been passed on by the commissioning client to be viewed by a board of directors, a parent company, an investor, or a brand compliance team; any one of whom could then request alterations to a job that could legitimately have been considered complete. This is especially true of multinational businesses.

Okay. I must have made all this sound like a nightmare. But really, it is not that bad. There can be a positive side to such corporate bureaucracy. Organisations with complex internal affairs frequently require their suppliers to jump through many hoops, and attend seemingly needless meetings with people who do not at first appear to justify any involvement. However, your client will usually be only too aware that their organisation's inner workings will be difficult for outsiders to fathom. Taking the time to really understand the way their business operates, and accepting all its associated eccentricities, can gain you a place in the "inner circle" of trusted suppliers. Minor suppliers who do not make the effort to understand the workings of their clients' businesses, or cause additional work for the client, risk becoming replaceable commodities. You want the client to feel you are a part of *their team*, and to become a trusted confidante.

One final note on working with clients who operate by committee: Always factor extra time into your estimates for revisions to the finished work. The more cooks there are in the kitchen, the longer it usually takes for a final sign-off to be agreed.

Keep track of where you spend your time

It can be helpful to track the hours you work on a project. Primarily, this is a good way to make sure you are not underestimating—or overestimating—your time commitments when costing projects. We implemented a period of time-tracking a few years ago when we got a nagging feeling we were putting in far more work than we were charging for. As a result, we found our estimates for time commitments on shoots, outgoing expenses, and post-production were for the most part highly accurate. However, we were significantly underestimating the amount of time we were spending on project management: Planning the logistics of a project, making calls, drafting emails, the hours spent in client meetings, and our travel.

There are many project management apps that incorporate time-tracking. Many apps have more features than are necessary, so I use a simple time-tracking website named Toggl. It has a desktop and mobile app with a simple button that I tap at the beginning and end of every task, at the end of each week I get an email with a summary of the hours I have spent on a project or client basis. Don't get sucked into becoming a productivity nut and getting so tied-up in time-and-motion studies that your creativity takes a hit; but tracking your time for even just a couple of weeks can give great insights as to where your time and energy are being spent, and whether you're billing for all of it.

Some clients also work in a similar fashion, and will call you at intervals to ask, "How many hours have you spent on this project so far, are we still within budget?" It is professional to be able to swiftly provide accurate figures. We give some clients a quick "end of week summary" of what we have been doing for them during the week. They usually have someone to report to at their end, and it saves them a call to chase for a progress report if we keep them in the picture before they even ask. It is just another small attention to detail you can implement to help make your client's life a little easier.

Sometimes your client's other projects, their annual holiday, or their kids' school terms can cause communication from them to go quiet. A quick email to run through the work you have completed and the deadlines you're still working to meet—even if there's nothing visual to show yet—can be a re-assurance that you're still progressing things in their absence. Do not be the supplier that always has to be chased for answers. Being elusive creates additional work for your client, and radio-silence can be unnerving.

Keep communicating, even after the job is done

I have made clear the importance of impeccable communication throughout a project. I should also point out the benefits of keeping lines of communication open *after* a project is complete. While working on a project, make sure you have been gathering useful intelligence on your client. When are their busiest periods? When do they do product launches? When do they decide on their annual marketing budget, and when is the end of their financial year? Do they have an annual conference or incentives scheme? If you can acquire this information, you will always have good reason to get in touch with your contact and catch up with how things are going in their business. You will be able to contact them at just the *right* time when a video project might be in discussion. We have become so familiar with some of our clients' annual schedules that they thank us for getting in touch approaching an important date to remind them it is time to start thinking about this year's production.

Staying in touch with some clients is essential to avoid being forgotten! We have a long-term client who occasionally gets in touch to brief us on a project, as they have done for more than 30 years. Yet, despite our long working history, we have never managed to pin them down to a monogamous production relationship for any extended period. They will go "missing in action" for several years before returning with more work. They are in a volatile sector, and the company seems to change ownership rather frequently. As a result, their marketing department has a high churn of staff, and the collective memory of the business is quite short. The staff often do not have enough knowledge of historic relationships to get in touch with producers that their predecessors were happy working with; they often have no idea who produced many of videos they already possess. It can be difficult to maintain long-term relationships with businesses that are subject to such repeated overnight reinvention. In such cases you should *instead* take far greater interest in the *individuals* you have been working with. Keeping in contact with them personally (LinkedIn is great for this) means they can sometimes introduce you to whoever will be filling their role. Failing that, maintaining a good relationship with a contact can open new doors for you when they move into their new position. Influencer and content creator Jarry Lee endorses the personal touch to keeping client relationships active,

> Thank you notes or emails can go a long way. I personally like to spend time a couple times a year thanking businesses or clients who have

commissioned my work, which can also be a helpful reminder to them that I'm happy to continue doing work for them. I've gotten additional gigs just by sending these emails. Sending occasional updates if you've worked on a major project that you're proud of can also help maintain relationships.

In summary

- Some clients will enjoy the collaborative feeling of being involved; others will want to be reassured that you understand the objectives, then will leave you to complete the work. There is no correct way, remain flexible, and learn how they prefer to work.
- Mistakes happen due to poor communication. If people are not given the right information at the right moment, or remain silent when they should have said something, your project is going to get derailed. Make sure everyone is kept in the loop.
- Keep your communications precise, unambiguous, and actionable. Be clear whether you are asking your client for an opinion or a decision. Use bullet points. Instead of saying "midweek" or "on Friday," try to state precise times and dates.
- Clients might not always be the best communicators, so you must pick up the slack and maintain your own high standards. Your interactions with them must always be precise and unambiguous.
- Items on your to-do list must always be defined actions, not merely hopeful outcomes.
- Ask how your client wants to be kept up to date on progress, how is it best to communicate with them? Microsoft Teams, Zoom, an old-fashioned phone call? Are there any cloud-based tools they might like you to implement, such as a shared Dropbox?
- If your client is not especially comfortable with tech, accommodate whatever methods they find easiest. Do not force your preferred personal workflow onto them.
- Aligning your workflow and communications with the client's internal way of doing things can earn you their loyalty. Disrupting *their* established workflow to accommodate *yours* will mark you as an outsider, and thus an expendable commodity.
- Find out exactly who has the final say on decisions made during a project, you can avoid prioritising one person's requested alterations when you are sure they may be superseded by directions coming from your established point of contact.
- Allow extra contingency in your schedule when working with clients whose corporate hierarchy could slow the progress of a project. Lengthy chains of communication should be factored into your approval period.

- Tracking your time can reveal the true extent of the hours you invest. Some clients will inevitably draw more of your resources than others, and it can help to understand whether you are factoring a true reflection of the time commitment into your budget and schedule.
- When the job is complete, stay in touch. Keep a good relationship going. Anticipate their future needs. Maintaining open lines of communication allows you to always be in the right place at the right time when they next need to commission a production.

17 Approval and delivery

Version control and watermarking

Version control becomes important when your internal method of organisation is extended into your client's world; this will often start when you are providing your client with draft versions of a script, but it becomes essential when you begin to send initial rough edits and renders for their ongoing approval. I have covered the importance of keeping clients in the loop, but you should beware of causing confusion by information overload. One of the easiest ways to create unnecessary work for your client is to send approval copies of work in progress at stages of production where their feedback would be nonessential, or the work is at too early a stage for their input to be of much value. You likely take your creative abilities for granted, but when you present a client with something incomplete, they might not so easily be able to fill in the blanks. You will need to clearly walk them how to interpret a work in progress. Ask for their guidance on your specific queries while explaining the areas where their input is not yet required. If your production is lengthy, only send the section of video where their input is needed. Excluding unfinished content from approval versions—or adding placeholder text—can lessen the chances of the client coming back with a snagging list of "problems" that are simply just work in progress.

- Never leave black sections in a client approval. You will inevitably get the complaint, "I think there's something missing at this point." We insert a neutral grey frame with a line of text explaining what is missing, and whether it is something we still require the client to provide, e.g. *"Logo Goes Here: Charlie to supply Illustrator file."* It can be time-consuming to draft an email listing all the caveats to explain partially completed work. Inevitably, the video will be forwarded to people who do not receive the background info, or do not read the entire thread. Make sure your approval videos are largely self-explanatory.
- Enable the overlay of timecode whenever you export an approval from your edit timeline. Explain to the client that any alterations or comments must include the associated frame-accurate timecode. When clients are

left to reference the time as displayed in whatever app they are using to watch the approval, the times they provide often have a large margin of error that makes it a headache to interpret their requests.

- Watermark approvals with the name of the originating timeline in your edit software; also—the status of the production, the version number of the file you are sending (you will send several throughout the course of a project), and the date. Use a standard naming convention throughout the project, and make sure the name of the file is the same as the watermark baked into the video itself. Our naming convention for an approval might look something like this "Acme Corp – Safety Video – Initial Assembly_UNMIXED_V4.0_12–07–21." Do not dispose of any of the approval files, they will be useful as a quick reference when a client wants to reinstate something that appeared in an approval from several days earlier.
- For first-time clients it can be a wise precaution to not send any unwatermarked video files until your final invoice has been settled.

Establish a finish line before you start the race

Wrapping-up a production is also an important part of the process. You need to plan how to get each project over the finish line. Early in the production process—ideally at the commissioning stage—you must decide with the client exactly what the final deliverable items will be, and what specifications they must meet. We always establish a deadline for the completion of a production, this is most often not a specific date, but a window of about a week. The "wiggle room" (as we call it) allows for a small deviation from schedule to allow for inevitable delays to feedback and decision-making caused by the client's other priorities. No matter whether your deadline is a specific date or a delivery window, no project should operate on a "no urgency" basis. Productions without an endpoint risk losing momentum, forever getting kicked further down the road, because there is no urgency to get them completed. Open-ended projects also create a high likelihood the client will continue to drip-feed nonessential tweaks and changes. Always work to meet a defined completion date, whether the client has specified one or not.

Meeting immovable deadlines

Conference videos carry the most specific requirements because they form part of a larger, and carefully planned event. A video may need to be exactly two minutes long because that is the time which has been allocated in the running-order for the day, and that duration is non-negotiable. Conference work has often been the most stressful, as the deadline has always been immovable. Several times I have worked through the night to make something work when an eleventh-hour client alteration would have otherwise wrecked the schedule. Conference projects can be unforgiving, but they are often the ones that the client cares about getting right more than any other. Conference videos often launch new products or set the tone for the year ahead, they are almost always under a lot of scrutiny.

At the outset you need to understand what needs to be delivered and by when. Years ago, the only method we had to deliver finished productions to conferences was on videotape or DVD, so we'd need to have everything wrapped-up and mastered a couple of days in advance. A last-minute change could—and once did—require a motorbike courier to make a 200-mile dash with a substitute videotape on the day of the conference. With fast file-transfer it is easy to be lulled into a false sense of having plenty of time to spare. It can help to create a self-imposed deadline a couple of days ahead of the one stipulated by the client.

Check, check, and check again!

There is nothing more harrowing than receiving a dreaded "There's a problem" phone call, especially when the time to rectify an error is running short. Despite best efforts, life sometimes throws a spanner in the works! Here are several "learning experiences" that might spare you from some potentially awkward situations:

"We can't play the file!" This occurrence is almost always down to client error. At smaller events you will often discover there is not a conference staging team involved. The client has just hired a small venue and tethered a projector to a laptop. There is little you will be able to do to assist in such a scenario unless you are nearby—in which case head over and help them out! Ask the client to check playback *ahead* of the event on the equipment they will be using on the day of the event.

"The video is the wrong shape!" Until recently this was rarely a potential problem. Video was always 4:3 aspect ratio, later 16:9 ratio, and standard definition was the norm. Today things are infinitely more complex. Video production applications are entirely format agnostic, meaning they can create video in any given dimension and frame rate. I have often had to produce items for display at conferences or exhibition stands that are used in portrait (i.e. 9:16 ratio) or other weird shapes for multi-projector or digital signage applications. It is good practice to check whether your shooting or post-production process needs to be modified to create a nonstandard specification master. The organisers of events are usually able to provide specification sheets with their exact requirements, e.g. for giant custom-layout LED video walls. Get the correct information as early as you can, because it is frustrating to spend hours adjusting and re-rendering a complex motion-graphics sequence to fit a different aspect ratio to the one you had been working in.

"There's a typo!" Thankfully, I have made few spelling errors in my career, almost all of the production software I've used has had a live spellcheck feature to flag any glaring errors. However, when dealing with corporate clients you will find that some of the on-screen text requires industry jargon, acronyms, and abbreviations; all of which are easy to assume have been typed correctly. This is especially the case when the client has supplied the text to you; copy and paste is a huge timesaver, but it often allows typos to sail straight through the process unchecked.

Names and job titles are an easy thing to get wrong, especially if the client throws a substitute participant into your shoot at the last minute, or someone's been promoted—or sometimes even demoted—in the period between scripting and post-production. Remind the *client* to check all the text at the approval stage. But, to head-off most problems before they arise make sure you get the names spelt correctly on your call sheet and double-check with any on-camera participants on the day of the shoot that you've got the correct spelling of their name and title.

Always get someone else—preferably multiple people—to check the spellings throughout your production *before* you send it out to your client. You should make it a standard part of your production workflow to call on "fresh eyes" toward the end of a production. From years of experience in sitting in darkened edit suite for days on end I can tell you this: As you get closer to the finish line you'll begin to focus your attention on sweetening colour grades and mastering sound mixes—and you will fail to notice many of the smaller components you've seen hundreds of times before. If you did not spot a typo the first time you saw it, you are very likely to continue working for hours, even days, and still not register that it's hiding in plain sight. From a client's perspective typos can be an irritation especially if they are a recurring problem, i.e. you fix the typo they have spotted, and on the next approval you send over, they spot another one! Save yourself a headache and try to catch any typos (or for that matter, any other glitches you might have become blind to) before sending out approvals.

"It's great but..." This could prefix any variety of problem. Most of the concerns that could complete that sentence could most likely have been resolved before the client ever raised a concern simply by reviewing your production with someone other than the client before sending it out for approval. You will unavoidably find yourself becoming too close to a production to remain entirely objective. This is the reason authors give their manuscripts to a Proofreader. Do not worry, I have not been able to see the wood for the trees on many occasions. Heck, even big-shot Hollywood directors appreciate the need to step back from their creations and seek the opinions of others. You may well think the explanatory graphics sequence you've created is absolutely clear—but *you* have had the script for days, you have had the client talk you through it, and you've been looking at it coming together on the screen for 14 hours straight! Someone who has never seen the sequence before will soon let you know where it isn't working for them. Take all comments on board and make amends where necessary, third-party critique is often the most useful.

The snagging list

The work on your project has concluded. You believe you have nailed the perfect production, and the client is sure to *love* every second of it. You send a final approval over to the client, and head home for that celebratory dinner you have been promising yourself.

The following morning you open your inbox to a list of amendments, quibbles, and alterations; *pages* of them! There are even requests from people you did not know would be involved in the approval process. This is something that everyone in any kind of creative profession can immediately relate to. You have only two possible choices: Get irritated. Or, make it your chance to shine. Making alterations without fuss is another opportunity to show your client that you're happy to take their requests on board, and that when things aren't quite spot-on you can always find a creative solution to make things right.

First let me say this: It is rare for a client to be so delighted on their first viewing of your production that they sign-off a project without any alterations. Usually, it is not a reflection on anything you have done incorrectly. A paying client will almost always have alterations to make before final sign-off. During my entire career I can recall only a handful of times a client has given the thumbs-up on first viewing without requesting at least one small alteration.

Having to accommodate changes is an inevitable part of creating anything for money. Sometimes it can be a little demoralising to incorporate ill-conceived alterations to a creation you are proud of, but the key to happy clients is to always remain cooperative. Your client genuinely *does* know best, even if their interpretation of "best" differs from yours.

That said, where should the line be drawn? When is it okay to tell a client their requested alterations are not valid? At what point does it become necessary to explain that any further amendments to a project will be chargeable? We found we were able to manage the expectation of endless rounds of amendments by explaining to the client—at the outset of production—that the editing process would allow for *three* rounds of approval and amendment requests.

In summary

- Establish careful version control, watermarking, and naming conventions to make the approval process clear for the client. Sending a client an approval video without providing them with all the necessary context to understand what they are viewing will raise more questions than answers. Your approval videos should be self-explanatory, making clear which areas require the client's feedback and which areas can be overlooked at the current stage of production.
- Establish a deadline. Do not let a project run without a completion date, even if it is just within a window of time. Even "no rush" projects should be scheduled and actioned in the same manner as "urgent" ones.
- When you have an immovable deadline, set yourself a self-imposed completion date a couple of days ahead of the deadline the client has set, and try to stick to it. This will help prevent schedule creep and provide a buffer of spare time to accommodate genuinely urgent alterations.
- Check your own work, and then get *someone else* to check it. You are the very *worst* person to spot errors in your own work.

18 Doing it by the book

Copyright and attribution

If you take away only a single observation regarding copyright it is this: If you find yourself trying to rationalise and find justifications or loopholes for using something without permission or fees—you are most likely violating copyright law. If in doubt, always take the high ground, even if that means withdrawing from a project to protect your livelihood.

You will discover that some clients possess a cavalier interpretation of copyright. Their fallacies seem biased toward an assumed right that they can use whatever materials they wish in the promotion of their business. Contrary to popular belief, people *do* get bothered when their creative endeavours are stolen without attribution or financial remuneration. Today, *everything* has the potential to be shared on social media, so it is more likely that copyright infringements will be discovered. Yet, you will often—legitimately—need to incorporate the creative works of others within your own. You must arm yourself with a reasonable working knowledge of copyright to protect your client, and yourself, by acting properly. Most of the time, an infringement would be so obvious as to be immediately avoidable. Ripping a scene from a hit movie or using a chart-topping music track on a client's video would at best be a takedown request, or at worst a lawsuit—you know that, and I know that. But… infringement can easily slip under the radar when the stakes appear insignificant. This is an appropriate moment to provide you with an example:

> We were producing a series of videos for a trade body. The purpose of the productions was to encourage foreign investment into a sector with potential for growth. The PR agency coordinating the productions had arranged several days of filming with notable industry figures who would express their confidence in the initiative.

We shot all the interviews. So far, so good. After compiling the strongest soundbites, the trade body requested some additional footage to illustrate a point one the speakers had made. The PR agency agreed to source this and asked the business we had filmed with if they had any videos that could be used. Seeing the opportunity to feature even more prominently, the business readily agreed and sent over several productions they claimed to hold the rights to.

We incorporated the supplied footage and syndicated an approval version of the cut. A couple of days later the PR agency received a very irate call from the producer of one of the videos that had been provided to us—until that point without their knowledge or permission. Heated words were exchanged while the agency agreed terms to pay the scorned producer for the footage. With retrospective permission gained—and a deeply apologetic phone call—tempers were calmed without further proceedings. Thankfully, the project had only reached an approval stage at the time the infringement was spotted. Had the trade body released the videos publicly, there almost certainly would have been legal action taken by the copyright owner. The client did not appreciate the extra hassle, or expense. They did not bring the PR agency any further projects.

Copyright law is an interesting subject to read up on, yes *really!* Many myths surrounding copyright have gone mainstream—despite being wildly incorrect. Specific laws differ by country, but a great primer on the overarching principles of copyright can be found here: www.whoishostingthis.com/resources/copyright-guide/

Royalty-free production resources

You can almost entirely remove headaches regarding the use of copyright sources by simply *paying* for graphics, images, video, and audio that have been pre-cleared for commercial use. You don't need to negotiate fees or wait around for permission; you can just buy what you need and use it right away. I have found that 99% of the time I can obtain the sources I require from either Adobe Stock, Shutterstock, iStock, or Pond5. All of them offer relatively inexpensive subscription models, or one-off purchase of individual assets. My personal recommendation for royalty-free music is www.epidemicsound.com as they have a very diverse range of high-quality tracks. Epidemic's licensing terms are comprehensive and cover your productions for a multitude of uses. Their tracks can also be downloaded as "stems" which will allow you to duck the vocals or other elements of instrumentation for greater flexibility in further editing and remixing a track, and this flexibility is worth the subscription.

Client confidentiality

Confidentiality is of paramount importance to every healthy client relationship. Your clients need to have absolute confidence that their dealings with you—and the projects you work on—remain entirely confidential until you have jointly agreed what can, or cannot, be made public.

Social media makes it remarkably easy to blunder into a highly embarrassing—or even costly—mistake by inadvertently making public something which should have remained confidential. Remember, computers allow you to make much larger mistakes, with wider-reaching consequences, faster than ever before! It is a rookie mistake to believe that everyone is waiting with bated breath for every update you post about the current events in your business. Professionalism means you remain aware of your clients' commercial sensitivities and keep quiet about anything you are privy to during a project. For the most part, your social followers really could not care much less about your status updates. Even when posting with the very best of intentions you can unknowingly create an awkward social media gaffe. I have been guilty of needing to remove what I believed to be a couple of entirely innocuous comments from social profiles for reasons I really wouldn't have had any cause to consider when my fingertips were on the keyboard. Pause and think, for just a moment, before you either type or open your mouth in a conversation where you might be tempted to discuss the clients you are working with.

First: When you have had a promising meeting with a new client it can be tempting to flatter your ego by letting everyone know that you might be gaining a new client. It is natural to want to spill the beans on your success by posting a little teaser Tweet:

> Really productive meeting with @acmecorp Thanks for the great coffee, looking forward to exciting things ahead!

Well, guess what? You had not been told about the other two producers whose meetings followed yours. Now they know who they are up against. You have also put your potential client in an awkward situation because their current producer did not know they were in the firing line; they do now. Worse still, they wanted to work with you on a white-label basis where your involvement would not made known to their end clients. Congratulations—The final call from your potential client is an irate one telling you to remove the post and keep your mouth shut. They feel you are not someone who can work discreetly. When it comes to confidentiality, do not ever utter a thing until your client is happy to go public with your production and acknowledge your involvement.

Second: Don't jump the gun, *even* when the job has been completed. When you are proud of a job well-done it is tempting to share your work on YouTube or your Facebook page, or to start incorporating it in your show-reel. Let the client's schedule lead you on this one, never release anything into the public domain until the client has done so. You should wait until you have received their permission, or at least until they have shared your video on their own social profiles. Remember, once a video is online your client can see it too; more savvy clients often use Google Alerts and other social management tools to get tipped-off about mentions of their own brand name.

It is guaranteed not to go down well if you are discovered to be promoting a video before their own marketing team have even seen it. Patience is a virtue.

Useful reminder: When you are putting a video on YouTube or Vimeo as an example of your work it can be a sensible practice to initially set the sharing settings to "private." You will be able to share the link with your contacts and embed the video on your website, but it will not show up in others' search results or "recommended for you" videos. We changed many of our videos to "private" after several comments, and sometimes enquiries that were meant to reach our clients were reaching us instead. Our uploads had been outranking our clients, and so appeared higher-up the search results.

Don't irritate brands

Office politics are always in play within large organisations. It is not always clear to an outsider how something that appears entirely harmless can be received like a hand-grenade tossed in your client's office. It is polite professional etiquette to ask for permission from your client before using your relationship and productions as a promotional tool. Let a relationship with a new client get solidly established and a firm foundation of trust develop before you begin namedropping. If you are lucky-enough to be working with a well-known brand, politely address the matter of using the relationship for your own marketing and PR benefit. It helps to get formal guidelines from them. No matter how happy a large business might be with your services, they can become irritated when small suppliers begin shouting from the rooftop about what is—from their perspective—a minor and tenuous association with their brand. When the job is done, hold fire. Your work is not a self-promotional piece until the client is far along the road in using the production for their own purposes.

In summary

- You will be charging clients for your productions; therefore, any copyright works you include in your productions are being used for *commercial purposes*, i.e. you would be profiting from using someone else's work without their permission—which would make you entirely fair game for legal action.
- Always ask about the origins of any materials you are given to work with. Check that your client has written permission from the original copyright owners before you use any material in a production. A verbal "We've been told we can use it" is not enough.
- If you do not have *permission* to use it, do *not* use it. A particularly aggressive complainant can pursue everyone who had a hand in enabling copyright infringement to take place. So, if your client were to receive a chilling letter threatening a lawsuit, it is likely you would receive one too.

- Always pay to use legitimate royalty-free libraries to source footage, photography, graphics, music, and sound effects.
- Even if your client has not asked you to sign a Non-Disclosure Agreement (NDA), it is simply a professional courtesy to keep the details of your work with them entirely confidential. Always get the go-ahead from your client before you share anything on social media or go public about a project.
- If the client has given permission for you to share a video as part of your marketing efforts soon after production (when they too might be actively sharing it) make sure to set your YouTube or Vimeo upload to private. You will be able to share the video yourself, but it will not show up in searches and risk interfering with your client's campaign.
- Keep details of your business dealings and sensitive projects away from social media. If you want to share "behind-the-scenes" images of work in progress, collaborate with your client's social media team so that you can both benefit from the posts. Posting without considering the ramifications can easily escalate an innocent post into a headache you did not need. There is no need to broadcast hourly updates on the operations of your business.

19 Behaving like a pro

Professionalism is treating fellow producers gracefully

The video production industry is a crowded arena, and you will often have your toes trodden on by other production companies chasing the same clients as you. Because of the density of the community you will absolutely have to hold yourself to the highest standards of professional integrity. Even when you lose a pitch to a competitor, just take a deep breath, and move to the next opportunity. Public bemoaning, becoming an irritation to former prospects, or bad-mouthing the winning production company is deeply unprofessional. Even when a client chooses to work with someone else, you will likely cross paths with them again. You never know when you will find yourself collaborating with someone you have previously lost a pitch to. Be nice.

Large production businesses—those employing dozens of full-time staff—are very much the exception. A typical production company today comprises a handful of key creatives and planners who draw on the skills of a roster of freelance crew. Freelancers will almost certainly be working with most—if not all—of the other producers in your area. Freelancers frequently work with one another on projects. Thus, gossip travels at the speed of light around freelance production teams and anyone behaving like an ass will soon become a common topic for discussion. Always pay freelancers promptly, poor payers are avoided like the plague and your pencil bookings will not be held for long when someone operating their business more fairly needs to book the same date.

Professionalism is understanding your client's situation

Your client's business means the world to them, so take the time to thoroughly understand the nuances of how they function. One of the simplest ways to engage with a potential client, and maintain a strong ongoing relationship, is to take a genuine and deep interest in their business. It means a lot to them, and it should mean a lot to you also. Gaining a deep understanding of the inner functions, and even the office politics, of a client's organisation is essential when you aspire to undertake sizeable projects for them. Ask a lot of questions, make plenty of notes, learn fast, and—if possible—gain an understanding of the hierarchy within their organisation. A trusting relationship is going to earn you the privileged position of being kept "in the know" about an organisation's plans at an earlier stage than other suppliers. This detailed understanding of the fabric of a business allows you to produce better work that will require fewer amendments. Most importantly it lowers the potential for embarrassing incidents which could demonstrate to the client that you have not entirely understood their internal politics.

We produced a teaser video for the staff incentive scheme of a large retail brand, the rewards ranged from theatre tickets to luxury foreign holidays. A new CEO was at the helm, and in the pre-production meetings with the client's marketing team it was suggested that the CEO's first "public outing" should be to present the new rewards scheme to staff.

To fit with the luxury travel theme our creative concept was for the new CEO to present the introduction to the video from the comfortable seat of a private jet. He would announce some of the possible destinations that teams from the best-performing stores may be able to visit, and we would overlay this with attractive stock footage of tropical beaches; you get the picture.

We made enquiries and located a private jet on the tarmac at a nearby aviation company. We got the shots we needed and finalised the video, feeling it did a great job of conveying the luxury appeal of the incentives on offer—it looked great! The production was screened to the client's board for their final approval—to their unanimous horror. There was a backstory we had not been made aware of. Their new CEO had been an expensive gamble, brought in for their experience of floating companies on the stock market. Part of the strategy for the floatation would involve some restructuring of the business, possibly resulting in job-losses. So, a video showing the new boss being served champagne aboard a luxury jet was unlikely to be met with a positive reaction, in fact it was likely to cause a great deal of ill-feeling. The production was immediately shelved and quickly reshot at a more neutral setting.

Okay, that example is hardly a common scenario, and it is one of only two reshoots I can recall us undertaking during three decades of production. Nonetheless, it is an example of how the adoption of a commercial mindset will help you become sympathetic to the communications challenges that always exist inside large corporate clients. You will never be able to please everyone. There will always be viewers questioning why their employer has spent money on a video production when they feel the money could be better spent elsewhere. Of course, the operations of your client's business are none of your concern; but you should try to be clued-up on the current state of their business so you can meet the viewers where they are at. Would lavishly shot visuals in photogenic locations really be appropriate if it might be common knowledge the business is in a tight spot financially? A good understanding of the sensitivities of your client's intended audience can help you avoid alienating them with your creative approach.

Professionalism is leaving your ego at the door!

I may have gently poked fun at some anonymous former clients, so it is time to hammer home a message which will hold you in good stead: The client really is *always right*, even on the occasions they do not appear to be correct. You are producing videos for *their* business and *their* needs. Ultimately, they will always understand those requirements better than you—even if you suspect their requirements might be misguided.

Before jumping to the conclusion that a client is being unreasonably demanding or obstructive, consider *Hanlon's razor.* The old maxim states, "Never attribute to malice that which is adequately explained by stupidity." Your client is most probably not being deliberately difficult—and they are certainly *not* stupid—but they might not fully understand the creative process and the rationale behind one of your decisions. In which case, their behaviour might well be due to a communication failure on *your* part. Lastly, make sure it is not your *perception* that is at fault. Early in my career I would feel personally affronted when a client would question my work; *I* was the creative, *not them!* I would wrongly perceive the client to be at fault because my feelings had been hurt. Over time I learned to step back from my creations; I became far more *objective.* If anything, critique is a great opportunity to do some additional problem-solving and put even more skills to good use. Sure, I still wanted my work to retain its "artistic" integrity, but my clients remained in the best position to judge whether the production was meeting their objectives. However, if your client's feedback still genuinely seems at odds with what they are trying to achieve—and they're unable to give understandable justification as to why they want to pursue a course of action—there is the possibility they might be incorrect. Give them the benefit of the doubt and use some gentle diplomacy when you feel their ideas may be leading them off course. Explain the rationale behind your suggestions, and the reasons why your advice will get them back on track.

Unfortunately, there will sometimes come a point where—with a deep sigh—you may have to accept that your client is not going to take your advice on board. Tactfully point out that you care deeply about their business, and the goals they are trying to achieve, but that you feel they are shooting themselves in the foot with the changes they are pushing for. Put forward all your potential solutions in writing, along with your professional recommendations as to why their requests may not be the best course of action. Take a *lot of care* to not sound like you are moaning; laying the groundwork for an "I told you so" moment is *not* the purpose of this exercise. Noting your proposed solutions in writing is simply a courtesy to yourself. If someone were to later gripe that the production has not done what was required of it—or someone in the client's organisation points out flaws you had already highlighted—you can sleep soundly knowing that you defended your professional integrity.

Professionalism is not pointing fingers, and not burning bridges

Creative projects are highly subjective, and we creators invest a lot of ourselves into our work. Our deep personal connection to the project in hand can be tiring, and it can sometimes cloud our judgement. It is easy to lose objectivity without noticing it is happening. That is the nature of creative work. Take a step back and reassess before acting rashly to any critique. Make sure the problems that are causing the stress are not of your own making. Perhaps the true reason it feels like your client is asking for the earth is because you under-costed the job, promised too much, or underestimated how many revisions a project of such complexity might entail. You can—and will—make mistakes. If a problem lies on your side you must own it, sort it out, and learn from it, before you point the finger at a "difficult" client.

Before you read ahead, I will state one point clearly: If a client continually shirks payment or wants to work on terms that are going to cause your business financial stress or cash flow issues—dump them. It does not matter the impression they take away from getting booted, just turn away their work. It is not worth jeopardising your business to work with clients who dodge invoices. That point made; I have read many articles advising small businesses and freelancers to "fire" clients merely for asking for a lot of their time, for not listening to all the advice they are given, for making "unreasonable" requests, etc. Well, sorry, but that's business. Dumping anything less than *perfect* clients seems to have become almost fashionable advice, and it is often raised in articles about minimising stress or avoiding burnout. I have seen template breakup emails to send out to errant clients at the first sign of stress. I have reservations about acting on drastic advice in the heat of the moment, "fire the client" paints a far too idealistic image of how to manage business relationships. In such articles, many of the examples of the "red flags" and "warning signs" purported to indicate a relationship is heading off-track are (from the perspective of someone who has worked with many seemingly "difficult" clients) often amicably resolvable with a tactful phone call, an email to clarify the next actions, even just a lunch to reconnect with them at a personal level. Yes, I sound old-school, but none of the articles I have read made mention of the potential repercussions of firing-off a *Dear John* message to a client, especially when they had no forewarning that something in the relationship was becoming problematic. Pulling the plug on a client where the "red flag" or "warning sign" could—in all honestly—be due to your own miscommunication or lack of appreciation of the client's way of working can blow up in your face. I would urge caution and some critical introspection before telling any client to get lost.

Sadly—only very occasionally—your hand can be forced, and you really are left with no option but to decline further work from a client. Once that bridge is burned there is often no way to rebuild it. Pulling the rug from under a client when the going gets tough is undoubtedly going to come across as unprofessional and leave a bad taste; you are not going to walk away from it without damage to your own reputation. There is no way they will be telling anyone that they were the ones at fault. We have only had to decline further work a handful of times, and that was only when a relationship had become entirely unworkable, or invoices were not being settled promptly. If you really do not want to take any further work from a client, complete the project you are working on (if that's a realistic option), wait for your invoice to be paid, and then let them move on. Try not to be the party who unexpectedly drops a client mid-project when they were not even aware that you were unhappy with the way things were working.

In summary

- Do not moan about anything. Whining is unprofessional and off-putting to clients. Period.
- The media industry relies on freelance specialists. Word spreads fast among freelancers, so your reputation matters when you want to book the best talent. Be enjoyable to work with, treat people fairly, and settle invoices promptly.
- Professionals plan for a long-term relationship with their client right from the start. Begin learning about your client's business from day one. Make sure the client appreciates that you want to get to understand their business so that you can serve them better.
- The client is always right, even on the occasions when they might not be.
- Before you decide a client is being unreasonable or obstructive, consider that their corporate priorities will differ from your creative vision. Are you being truly objective? Check whether your perception of the situation has been clouded by your personal feelings.
- Sometimes you *will* have to do what the client wants, despite your professional guidance. Often, when presented with what they wanted, they will sometimes appreciate the merits of your proposed course of action. Gracefully leave the door open for your client to come around to your solution.
- If a client is causing you financial disruption or creating bogus reasons to delay payment, it is professional of you to dispatch of them as a client. You do not need such headaches.
- Complex projects and demanding clients are a daily part of business operations, that is life. Before taking the drastic step of dropping a client who feels too arduous to work with, be brutally honest with yourself: Had you done *everything* you could on your side to make the relationship operate more smoothly?

- If you do get stuck with a client that is genuinely exceptionally disruptive, explain the situation, and—if you are able—complete the project to the client's satisfaction and end the relationship amicably. Do not leave a bad taste. People move on, teams change, and hellish clients can have their corporate cultures transformed under new ownership. If you were giving the client your best it is likely someone at their organisation *was* on your side and enjoyed working with you. Try not to burn bridges.

20 Managing your tech

Mac or PC?

To this point, you thought I was an alright guy. Now, 50% of you just decided you hate me! Why on earth would I raise such a contentious area of debate?

For more than 20 years I have had a foot in both camps and split my time between Macs and PCs. I have managed both Apple and PC hardware on the same network inside the same business, and the world has not stopped spinning because of my heresy. So, why am I writing about a non-issue? Well, it is just to make you aware of a historical precedent. In the 1980s the Macintosh computer was leaps ahead of the PC in terms of its graphics capabilities, so design software was primarily released for Mac, and advertising agencies purchased Macs for press layout. When non-linear (computer-based) editing began to replace videotape editing, Avid built their editing system on Apple hardware. If you worked in a creative business, you bought Macs; there was not much choice in the matter. In the intervening years, the power of PC hardware rocketed, and Microsoft upped its game. Applications are now largely cloud-centric and function seamlessly across multiple devices and operating systems.

So, whether you decide to operate your production company on PC or Mac—or even both—is entirely down to your own preference. What user interface will you prefer to use all day long? Whichever route you choose, purchase the very best hardware you can afford. Unlike other production equipment, your computer is *undoubtedly* going to be a piece of kit you spend most of your time using. When you are using your computer for everything from client emails and Zoom calls to editing and motion graphics, that computer is quite literally the *home* of your production business! Yes, I urge you to have a conservative spending policy in all other areas of your business, but do not cheap-out on IT. If you ever catch yourself saying to someone "Sorry, my computer is on a bit of a go-slow right now" you need to upgrade it as soon as possible! You need the fastest, most optimised, and most resilient hardware you can get hold of.

Always have at least two backups

Data loss is a catastrophic blow for any business, but especially so for a video production company. The media we shoot, and the enormous quantities of additional data we create during post-production are *mission critical*. Lose the data, and you lose the production, and most likely your client with it! I cannot stress the importance of building ridiculously paranoid data redundancy procedures into your production workflow.

Our data requirements have rapidly raced to a whole new level of technical and logistical complexity. When you have completed your first handful of productions, you will unavoidably begin to reach the limitations of your data storage. Our standard lineup of cameras today is either RED, Amira, Alexa, or comparable Sony and Canon equivalents—a lot of cameras, creating a hell of a lot of data! It is not uncommon for the team to return from a shoot with anywhere from 500GB to more than 1TB of footage. All this media needs to be immediately cloned before leaving the filming location, and this first backup stored off-site. Thus, immediately at the end of the filming the data—at the very least—doubles, and in post-production the data will likely double yet again. The longer you continue to operate without a data management strategy in place, the greater the damage when something does inevitably go wrong. Start as you mean to go on and get your data storage, backup, and retrieval processes in place from the outset. Things will go wrong, and data will get lost—it is not a question of *if*, but *when*. Make sure there is always at least two backups in place.

RAID: Redundant Array of Independent Discs. RAID is a mature storage technology that enables hard discs (and now Solid State Drives (SSDs)) to be ganged together as a single virtual drive. This provides faster read and write speeds which are essential for the playback and editing of multiple streams of video at 4K resolutions and beyond. Different RAID configurations can provide varying degrees of redundancy, allowing a disc in the set to fail without taking your data with it. RAID can keep your data safe for the period you are replacing a failed disc, but never consider it to be a backup in the truest sense. RAID is simply a layer of defence in a larger plan. Your data can still be deleted, stolen, or otherwise destroyed, and the hardware that operates a RAID array can also fail. Always consider the worst possible scenario that could happen and plan to avoid the consequences.

As a first line of redundancy, we do not *ever* leave a day's shoot without first having copied the camera's memory cards onto a portable SSD. The drive travels back to base separately to the cards. Back at base the footage on the cards is copied onto the RAID storage of the post-production suite that will be working on the project. So, before work on the edit gets underway there will already be *three* copies of the footage. Each of our edit suites is set to automatically copy their contents to a shared SAN (Storage Area Network) array at the end of each working day, creating a *fourth* copy. There are numerous free and paid utilities to do all this, and automation is key to making sure the creation of regular backups is not overlooked. Our backup SAN is kept in a keypad-entry server room far away from the production suites. It is possible to have systems which maintain a continuous mirror of your data, continually keeping your computer and remote storage synchronised.

However, this seemingly failsafe method of backup can unravel when human error is involved. Delete a file by accident on your computer, and it immediately vanishes from the backup device too. Keeping daily backups provides a few hours' grace period to retrieve a lost file. Cloud storage is steadily becoming feasible for the backup of production media. Newer 5G mobile networks have the potential to get the data to the cloud far faster than conventional wired internet. Cloud storage also benefits from version control, so you will be able to roll files back to an earlier state should you need to. It is an area of technology I watch with great interest; it may seem like doom-mongering, but you should seriously consider whether your production business could be wiped-out by a fire or the theft of your computers, or just simple human error.

You will probably be starting out with a more modest setup, so your backup procedure can be as simple as a couple of high-capacity SSD drives that you swiftly copy your projects onto—in duplicate—at the end of your day. Remove the drives and put them somewhere a long way from your computer. Your data is the most critical asset your production business will own. Your clients have paid for all the work that went into creating that data, and they expect it to be kept safe. If you lose it, you must recreate it at your own cost, assuming it is something which can be recreated. Once the data has gone, all the future revenue from that client—in the form of recuts and alternative future usage of that material—goes along with it.

Lesson 1: A single backup is *never* enough. In the event of a data loss your backup—by default—becomes the only copy of your data in existence. So, no backup is truly a backup unless it is done in at least *duplicate*. As the Navy SEAL maxim wisely states, **"Three is two, two is one, and one is none."**

Lesson 2: Until you have verified that your backups can be recovered in their entirety, you simply do not have an adequate backup regime. Merely assuming all has gone well, or not being prompted by any sort of error message, is not *any* kind of reassurance. You must check that your data has copied in full and can be read back.

Lesson 3: Never, ever, ever, ever format your camera's memory cards until you have taken several copies. Just set the cards aside and keep them somewhere safe, ideally off-site, until the production is complete. Recording media and drives are relatively inexpensive, so buy enough of them to last you through several weeks of production before you need to begin wiping and reusing. It's too easy to believe a copy of footage has been taken before letting a camera go out on its next job, and that scenario is especially likely when you're sharing equipment, are using rental gear, or have several productions overlapping. You do not want to find yourself on a shoot, with five minutes of storage left, and be in the position of struggling to recall which memory card in your bag will be okay to wipe first. The memory cards in your bag should *always* be blank, formatted, and ready for immediate use. Cards with footage on them need to stay securely shut away at base until they can confidently be returned to use. A common solution used by Camera Assistants is to use fluorescent camera tape to seal each memory card in its case at the very moment it is removed from the camera, leaving no one in any doubt that it has essential footage on it. Keep the case taped shut until the card can be returned to use.

Archival of projects

For many decades, the archival of video productions was a relatively low-tech affair. An archive was comprised of lots of shelving, hundreds of video cassettes, and a card-index. Any additional information about a tape could just be written on the box. Simpler times.

As your list of clients begins to grow, the long-term archival of your projects will soon become a consideration; not least when your drawers and cupboards have become packed with assorted hard drives and associated cables and power adapters. For deep-archival purposes we use LTO6 Ultrium tape cartridges, these archival-grade tapes have an estimated shelf life of 40 years. LTO tape is not an inexpensive solution, but as with all backup considerations it's a case of weighing up the current and potential future value of your data (and costs associated with losing any of it) versus the cost of maintaining thorough and reliable backups. On very substantial projects—those that accumulate hundreds of gigabytes, even terabytes, of footage—the cost of archival tape and secure storage is factored into the cost of the project. If hard discs or SSDs are your *only* solution early in your business, always do backups of your projects in duplicate, or even triplicate. Cheap and expensive drives alike will all suffer catastrophic failure eventually. I will repeat that wise maxim again, **"Three is two, two is one, and one is none**."

Side note: Back in the days when hard discs were ludicrously expensive, I would archive work on CD-R and DVD-R discs. On a few occasions that clients required me to revisit old projects I discovered that many of the discs had faded and become unreadable after only a handful of years. Although writable optical discs are now almost entirely defunct, I am wary of storing critical material on any medium not specifically created for enterprise-grade long-term archival. Thankfully, the original footage for the projects on those faded discs had remained accessible on videotape, which had weathered the sands of time just fine.

Make sure your working methodology leaves no single point of failure for footage loss to *ever* become a possibility.

Asset management

In your early months it will be possible to keep track of all your production equipment, memory cards, USB sticks, and drives associated with the work you produce. For a while you will be able to remember what stuff you own, and where it is all kept, especially if you are still working alone. Your whole business can probably all fit in the drawer of your desk. However, the amount of "stuff" you are responsible for will quickly begin to grow exponentially.

The production company I am currently with launched in 1983. Over the decades it has accumulated hundreds of items of equipment, several thousand videocassettes, almost 100 hard drives, and—at the time of writing—67 LTO Ultrium data tapes containing *millions* of files. We carefully label and catalogue all these items with pre-printed asset ID tags. Asset tags are no more than pre-printed adhesive "property of" labels that have our name and a unique number on each. Whenever you acquire a new item that should remain within your business, stick a tag on it and add its number and a description of the item to a spreadsheet. If the item has a serial number, put that on the spreadsheet too. If you need to loan something to a client—a hard drive for instance—make a note on your spreadsheet of the item's current whereabouts.

In summary

- Choose post-production systems for speed and reliability above all else, but also to suit your own preferences and ease of use. You will be spending most of your time running your business from your computer, so make sure you are happy with it.
- Be conservative in all areas of spending in your business, but do not underspecify IT equipment to save a small amount of money. Buy the best you can. Shaving minutes off processor-intensive tasks adds up.
- *Three is two, two is one, and one is none.* Always keep your data stored in *triplicate.* Hard discs fail. Be paranoid. Do not sleep at night until you have multiple copies of everything. The cost of storage hardware and tape backups is minimal in contrast to the amount of financial and reputational damage you can do to your business by losing project assets.
- Never *assume* your data has been copied, you must check it. You can also use checksum utilities to compare and analyse copies for errors.
- Buy enough memory cards so that you never have to wipe them during an active project.
- Plan for the long-term archival of your projects. Could you reliably retrieve all the footage and production data for a client in five, or even ten years from now?
- Keep track of all the equipment, gadgets, and storage media that you purchase by labelling them with pre-printed asset ID tags. Maintain a spreadsheet of all your assets and their whereabouts.

21 Managing your finances

Tilman J. Fertitta is an American businessman with a net worth of approximately $4.5 billion. In an interview with CNBC in 2016 Fertitta said the one piece of advice he would give to every young entrepreneur is, "Don't ever let your business get ahead of the financial side of your business. Accounting, accounting, accounting. Know your numbers." I cannot disagree with a guy who has that many digits attached to his name! And, if you have seen the TV show Dragon's Den (aka Shark Tank) few things anger the panel of investors so much as wannabe entrepreneurs who are clueless about their revenue, manufacturing costs, or overheads. Their annoyance is well-founded; business owners with little grasp of their own accounts are often heading towards trouble.

Regardless of how impressive your roster of clients, or how busy you are with a continual flow of projects, your production company's finances will *never* take care of themselves. It is not unusual for good businesses with happy clients to find themselves with serious money problems, either because they find business finances intimidating or, quite simply, not a high priority. Being busily occupied by client projects every day can provide a false sense of security.

Be brutally honest about your financial abilities

Right. Brace yourself for a sweeping generalisation: Creative people can become absorbed in their craft to the extent they become blinkered to the financial implications of their decisions. There, I said it—and I am not sorry. Early in the book I stated that building a production business would require you to develop a *broad* range of knowledge in addition to your depth of *creative* skills, i.e. to acquire a rounded and complementary set of abilities. You do not need to become an accountant to manage your production business, but you will need a solid grasp of fundamental accounting principles and a change in the mindset you have toward money. If you often have no idea why your personal bank account is empty at the end of the month, we still have much work to do!

Jason Cherubini recounted to me the story of a freelance producer establishing himself as a business to expand his offering,

> When he was first setting up the business, we met to discuss what he would need to do in order to keep track of everything and be compliant with all of the laws. We discussed things like payroll, and bookkeeping, and government filings. To each of these things we discussed, he responded with something like 'I can handle that'. This producer is very talented. He is great with the crew, with agents, and with talent. He has helped structure very large and complicated projects. But he also regularly gets notices that the electric company is going to turn off his lights because he forgot to pay the bill. His mind does not focus on those details until they become problematic. What I suggested he do—and thankfully, he took this advice—was to hire a bookkeeper to keep track of his expenses and make sure the business bills get paid. He also outsourced all of his payroll and tax preparation so that these were all taken care of.

Before you pay yourself, pay your business!

One of the most basic rules of managing your corporate finances is to remember that your business needs to earn and retain money. Channelling profits back into your business bolsters it with the stability to ride out bumps in the road, and to accumulate capital for you to invest in the further growth of the business. Jason highlighted a key concept that production company founders must appreciate,

> A business is separate from its owner. It needs to survive and grow. If you are transitioning from a freelancer to a business owner, you need to realize that the money the business earns is not yours. The money first needs to keep the business going and growing. What's left after that can go into your pocket.

As a cautionary tale, Jason told me about a multiskilled freelancer who decided to draw his skills together into a single business offering,

> He decided to start a production services business, offering up his own skills, the rental of his gear, and subcontracting of other freelancers through his company. Due to his natural artistic talents, he had always been sought after on productions and that continued when he began his business and he was doing well. The problem was that he continued to think of himself as a freelancer, so with every new contract that came in, every penny that wasn't paid out to his subcontractors he took for himself. He didn't keep any of the profit in the business, and he didn't spend any money to grow the business. Despite not spending money to grow

> the revenue of the business, the expenses of the business grew. All the software, and subscription services and backups cost money, and many were on annual contracts. Regretfully, the state where this individual did most of their business put an end to a film tax credit and the demand for his work dried up. Because he had never invested to grow the business outside of that state he had to quickly try and pivot. This was complicated because no money had been left in the business, having all being spent by the individual, so the business quickly ran out of funds and the bills kept coming.

The current entrepreneurial style is to "scale fast," "pivot," "be a unicorn," etc. Well, it is a lot easier to leap from one strategy to another when you are playing with someone else's money. Investing profit back into the development of your own business will require control, patience, and a long-term outlook. When you are creating your own company, you will watch friends climbing their own career ladders and likely earning more than you. Becoming an overnight success story often takes years of hard work. Jason agrees,

> If you are going to start a business, you need to start taking a longer view than if you are working as a freelancer. The business will require planning and investment to flourish. This will mean that in the near-term, you are taking home less money than if you were just working as a freelancer, but all of that investment and effort means that as the business grows, you will be able to earn significantly more than any individual could make freelancing.

Bookkeeping and payroll: Who should do what?

Calculating production estimates, invoicing of projects, and daily cash flow management should remain entirely your responsibility. These are basic financial bookkeeping requirements that you need to stay on top of. Kicking daily financial chores down the road in the hope the books will magically balance at the end of the month will cause problems to build unnoticed. That said, even though you are managing the business, serving your clients will place great demands on your time. So, while you must understand the *principles* of business financials, an accountant can be tasked to manage monthly payroll, official tax filing, preparation of forecasting, and financial analysis. Jason Cherubini adds,

> Unless it is something they have a knack or passion for, it is usually in the small business owner's best interest to hand-off as much of the record keeping as possible. This is especially true with things like Payroll and Taxes where the cost of paying a professional to do is far lower than the potential costs if there is a problem. But, handing over the official record keeping does not mean that the business owner can 'set it and forget it'.

> They should still *review* all documentation and *understand* what the numbers are saying, they are just handing off the routine entry and filing steps. Every business owner needs to understand and apply themselves to the evaluation of projects. This means going through the steps to forecast revenues and costs to ensure that a project is going to be profitable for the business, and that during the project costs are kept in check.

Intuit Quickbooks, Sage, and Xero are the most popular—but certainly not the only—online business accounting platforms. For a small monthly fee (you probably spend more on coffee each month) they can handle the hard maths for you—you just input your financial data (the bookkeeping). All the platforms allow you to search for an accredited accountant by postcode/zip. You can grant the accountant collaborative access to your account, then hand off whichever aspects you are less knowledgeable about, or find too much of a time-suck. Don't underestimate the value of having a pair of experienced eyes regularly checking your accounts and able to offer professional advice.

Forecasting and analysis

It is critical to understand the importance of financial forecasting. A lack of forecasting can cause a company's owners to be unaware of the trajectory of their finances—oblivious to a creep in their overheads, maybe a drift toward less profitable projects, the effect of taking on a finance agreement, or the long-term expense of new member of staff. A business will also accumulate small outgoing expenses, gradually making it less profitable; just the same as gym memberships and small subscription payments deplete your personal bank account without you even noticing. When the profits from your projects are being invisibly swallowed by the costs of doing business, forecasting will give you advance notice that your business is on a road to running out of cash. Forecasting will also provide ample time to anticipate annual expenditure such as software licenses, taxation, or insurance policy renewals—no expense should ever come as a surprise.

Invoicing

Settlement of invoices can become a sore point of any client relationship. No matter how much you enjoy working with your client, sluggish payment or repeated chasing of their accounts department can tarnish relationships. As much as you might enjoy working for the client, their accountancy team will often be far removed from the project, and likely do not know who you are—so, unfortunately, your stellar reputation will often not count for much. Continually pursuing some clients to pay within your stated terms is something that will inevitably affect your fledgling production operation as much as any other business. It is nothing personal, slow payers are a fact of life—not everyone will be managing their cashflow as well as you surely will.

However, you can strive to make sure any delays at the payment stage are not of your own making. Make sure your invoices are correct and meet your client's requirements.

Invoice in stages

You should always invoice a new client for a commissioning payment prior to committing your time to significant amounts of work. You can, of course, begin planning the project but be careful not to incur any outside expenses until the commissioning invoice has been settled. For small projects we typically invoice 50% of our estimate upfront. For larger commissions (or projects likely to occupy us for several weeks) we usually break our invoices into three, or even four stages. Whatever the percentage, your first invoice should cover all your immediate outgoing costs and the time you anticipate dealing with the project up to the date when you anticipate the next invoice to be dispatched. The objective is to ensure that if the client bales out—or even goes out of business—you are unlikely to be made significantly out of pocket.

Your client will often ask about your payment terms at the briefing stage. If they do not ask, then you should raise the subject and let them know that a commissioning payment is standard for new clients. We have rarely had any pushback from clients on this, they understand that at the start of a project we will often have some immediate outgoing costs to cover. Very occasionally you might be told, "No one has ever asked me to pay up front! Don't you trust me? There's no way I would ever agree to that!" Do not take this to heart. The moment it gets inferred you are being money-grabbing or a con artist for legitimately asking for a partial commissioning payment you need to decide whether you want to continue with the client. They have just set the tone for the rest of the working relationship; you will likely be chasing the money for ages—if they pay at all. Tell them you are grateful for the opportunity, but your terms of working are clear, so on this occasion you will have to decline the work.

Make your payment terms clear at the outset

You are the one running your business, so you can set the terms for your payment—within reason. You cannot specify to be paid the very next day, or to only accept payment in gold bullion, but requesting payment to be made within 30 days of the invoice being issued will be commonplace for many of the clients you will work with. For commissioning invoices, you should be able to get agreement from the client to request shorter payment terms of 7 or 14 days, or even payment by return if the client wants you to begin work on a project immediately.

As a side note, check whether your client also works to 30-day terms as early as possible. It could be the case that your client is owned by a far larger organisation, and some major corporations demand extended 60-, 90-, or even 120-day payment terms. For small businesses, that can be an unacceptable burden on cash flow, and you might not want to work under those terms. One of our clients is a manufacturer in an industry with exceptionally long payment terms (120 days) but our contact was able to do some negotiating on our behalf to move us to a list of "accredited suppliers" and make clear to the accounting department that we were a marketing expense and not a supplier of manufacturing components, i.e. the product of our work is put to use far sooner than the products coming off the production line, so the 30-day terms on our invoice should be met.

You are also within your rights to specify that you charge interest for every day your invoice remains unpaid beyond your specified due date. Check out the *Late Payment of Commercial Debts (Interest) Act*. Specify your terms, including interest on late payments, to your client—always in writing—at the outset of the project.

Before drafting your invoice, ask your client about their standard terms of payment for suppliers. They might require you to obtain a purchase order number, or perhaps they make all their outgoing payments on the same date each month, meaning you will need to get your invoice to them before a cutoff deadline. Perhaps most important of all, who do you send the bill to? We do not invoice all our clients directly, some of them require invoices to be sent to the accountancy team at a larger parent company.

Why extending a line of credit to a client is a bad idea

We had been involved in the marketing campaign for a major commercial property venture. We were briefed to produce a video to market retail spaces in the proposed development, the intention was to find a major anchor tenant to sign a lease that would get construction underway. The video would rely heavily on 3D visualisations of the finished units. The client had already engaged another business—specialising in the production of architectural walkthroughs—to design and render the 3D elements. We were tasked with writing a script, producing a soundtrack, and doing the post-production to pull all the pieces together. Newly formed ventures throwing lots of start-up capital at launching something that does not yet exist can be risky clients, they are often gambling with taps of money that could be turned off at any moment.

As standard, we asked for 50% upfront from this new client, and progressed with the work once the commissioning invoice had been settled. We incorporated all the stunning 3D visuals, got sign-off on the video, and sent our final invoice. The 30 days came and went, we chased for payment daily, we progressed to hints of legal action, and eventually we passed the account to our solicitor. The client had gone bust, their offices abandoned. Painful, unpleasant, and a kick in the teeth—but all our outgoing costs, and much of our time, had been covered by our initial 50% invoice. The demise of the client had wasted our time and effort, but our outgoing costs had been covered by our first invoice, we owed money to no one. We were able write off the sum of the unpaid closing invoice without losing sleep over the financial implications.

The sad part of the tale: The CGI business that had designed—and already completed—the 3D walkthroughs had fared far worse. They had taken the project on trust and asked for no money at the outset. A team of designers had been working for weeks on the project, and their full £14,000 invoice went unpaid.

Invoice quickly, invoice clearly

There is no single acceptable template for an invoice, but countless desktop and mobile apps (including those associated with the accounting platforms mentioned earlier) can format your invoices correctly, you simply fill the correct information. The essentials you will need to make sure are present on all your invoices are:

- Your name and address.
- The name and logo of your business if you are trading as such.
- Your company number (if you are a Limited company).
- Your VAT number (if registered).
- Registered office address, which may be different to the address your business is located.
- The name and address of your client.
- Any purchase order or specific project reference supplied by your client.
- A description of the work that you have completed for the client, what has been delivered, e.g. "Production of marketing video for new line of widgets." If appropriate, detail how many billable hours you accrued on the project, and any additional items that were not in the original estimate, e.g. "One overnight stay due to shoot overrun."
- Your bank details (account number and sort-code) for BACS transfers. If you issue an invoice via a cloud-based accounting platform you might also have other options such as accepting card-payments.
- The date. This is *very* important as the date you put on your invoice is the date from which the countdown to your payment due deadline begins.
- Your terms and conditions, specifically stating *when* payment is due—e.g. "Payment must be made within 30 days from date of invoice."
- Lastly—this might sound obvious—make sure the word "Invoice" is prominent. You do not want your client to misunderstand that you have sent a request for payment!

In summary

- Invoice new clients for a commissioning payment. A legitimate client should not object to paying a percentage of the project's cost before work begins. You must mitigate against finding yourself at a loss should the client walk away from the project or fail to pay the next invoice.

- On complex, or lengthier, projects you should invoice in staged payments. This is especially important if you are subcontracting any areas of the project or will begin incurring expenses from the outset. Staged invoicing not only lowers the risk to your business, it can also aid your cash flow by bringing in regular smaller payments throughout the project.
- Gain a good understanding of the fundamentals of business accounting—especially cash flow forecasting, and profit and loss forecasting. Businesses find themselves in financial difficulties when they owe more money out more than they have received in. Even a business making profit on the work they do can struggle because their money is in the wrong place at the wrong time.
- Business accounting *can* be enjoyable. Honest. Understanding your business' financial position is empowering. Knowing the numbers gives you control and allows you to make informed decisions. Seeing your profitability laid out on a spreadsheet will give you additional confidence that your decision-making skills are sound.
- You do not have to prepare financial analysis yourself. If accountancy isn't in your skillset, you can leave preparation of spreadsheets and forecasting to an experienced accountant. However, you must be able to *understand* what the data *means*, and what actions you should take as a result.
- Maintain robust and conservative cash flow projections. Maintaining a good cash flow keeps your business operating smoothly on a day-to-day basis, and make sure you still have cash in the bank at the end of the month.
- Longer-term profit and loss forecasting will show the trajectory your business is on. This forecast will show whether your business will continue to operate profitably in the coming months, or whether the business is on a slippery slope toward operating at a loss, or even failing entirely. Forecasting is essential, because it provides advance notice of what is ahead, and allows you to adjust your business operations to keep on the right track.
- If you can measure it, you can control it. Put another way, if you can predict when the poop is going to hit the fan, you can do something to intervene and stop it happening.
- Maintain a comfortable safety net of immediate cash. Accumulate a sizeable buffer of security—a "rainy day" fund—starting from day one. When a client fails and defaults on an invoice, or the economy falters and other production companies struggle, you will be better able to adjust your business and keep going because your cash will buy you time.

22 So, that's a wrap!

As a result of reading this book you're hopefully feeling confident and excited about expanding the horizons of your career, either as a freelance multiskilled producer, part of a collective of remote creatives, or with a view to setting up shop as fully staffed video production company. I sincerely hope you will be able to find the ideal balance between satisfying your creative talents and maintaining the healthy amount of scepticism and objectivity required to sell your skills for commercial ends. Your production business will be uniquely yours; it should reflect your values and your creative flair, and you should assemble a team around you who share those same values. I hope this collection of advice and professional anecdotes, from what feels like a lifetime in this business, prove useful to you.

Video production is a great line of work to be in, and—if you are already in the business—you will know that you get to work with a great bunch of people. Heck, even the people you will often be pitching against are nice folks who share the same interests and passions as you. Sure, you might not make as much cash as striking oil or inventing an infinite source of energy, but it is possible to make a rewarding and comfortable living in the video production business.

Moreover, you will be working in a career that provides a great deal of creative satisfaction and—dare I say—a life less ordinary. While other folks are working the 9-to-5, you will frequently find yourself as an "access all areas" guest in any number of interesting industries, and your projects might not be limited to within your own country. You *might* even be able to structure your production business in such a way that location is no object, you could become a global video producing nomad. The opportunities *are* out there. The greatest freedom of all is that you are the pilot, you can steer your production business in any direction you please. No two weeks will *ever* be the same, and you will grow a portfolio of work to be proud of; a showreel that can secure increasingly prestigious clients with larger goals, and just maybe larger budgets too. Good luck!

Index

Printed in Great Britain
by Amazon

22241160R00099